D1009041

Public Record Office Handbooks N

Tracing your Ancestors in the

by
Jane Cox and
Timothy Padfield

London: Her Majesty's Stationery Office

ISBN 0 11 440114 4

Frontispiece: Sketch in a General Register of Greenwich Hospital Pensioners. Early nineteenth century (ADM 6/322)

Contents

Abbreviations

MS   Manuscript

PCC   Prerogative Court of Canterbury

PRO   Public Record Office

TS   Typescript

Other letters are Public Record Office codes representing classes of records.

Introduction

The Public Record Office holds records of the government and the central law courts from the eleventh century and is a mine of genealogical information, but it is not the place to begin your research. There is no central index of names, and so the more you can discover about your family in advance the speedier and the more fruitful your researches in the public records will be. The PRO does not undertake genealogical research, except for specific records, for example wills, and then only if adequate information is supplied. Photocopies can be ordered by post if the documents are identified by the applicant. In all other cases you will have to obtain a reader's ticket and come to the search rooms to conduct your own research, unless you are prepared to employ a record agent (see VI below).

The Public Record Office has three repositories at present:

Public Record Office
Ruskin Avenue
Kew
Richmond
Surrey TW9 4DU
Telephone 01-876 3444

Public Record Office
Chancery Lane
London WC2A 1LR
Telephone 01-405 0741

Census Room of Public Record Office
Land Registry Building
Portugal Street
London WC2A 3HP
Telephone 01-405 3488

If you wish to consult the public records, you should ring the office at Kew to ascertain which repository you will need to visit. The search rooms are open to the public from 9.30 a.m. to 5 p.m., Monday to Friday, except on public holidays and during the first two weeks in October.

Records in the Public Record Office must be ordered by their call numbers, comprising group letters (e.g. WO, for War Office), class number (e.g. WO 97, for War Office, Soldiers' Documents) and piece number (e.g. WO 97/341, for War Office, Soldiers' Documents, 13th Foot, Abb-Car, 1760–1854).

The bibliographies contain, besides works for further reading and the names of the relevant record classes, information on various aids to finding and understanding the records. These can be in one of several forms:

  a Transcript: a full text, in which the abbreviations of the original manuscripts have been extended wherever this could be done with certainty.

  b Calendar: a precis, usually in English, full enough for most purposes to replace the original documents.

  c List: an enumeration of the units composing a class of records, with dates and simple descriptions.

  d Descriptive list: a list with brief abstracts of documents.

  e Index: alphabetically arranged references to people, places or subjects mentioned in the records.

  f Catalogue: a calendar or descriptive list containing records of similar content drawn from different groups or classes, sometimes for a special purpose such as a public exhibition.

It must be emphasised, that there is no single finding aid which gives precise references to all the records. Unpublished finding aids are to be found in the PRO unless otherwise stated.

Public records are normally closed for 30 years from the date of their creation. Exceptions to this rule are noted below.

There is a list of useful addresses given at the end.

The information contained in this handbook is correct as at the time of going to press, but certain items such as addresses of institutions, etc. and the services they offer may be subject to alteration.

1 For the beginner: preparation and method

Before searching original records, you must gather together any information that may already be in the family: oral tradition, pedigrees in family bibles, letters, diaries, etc. Always work backwards; it is very difficult to work forwards on the basis of a tradition that says you are descended from a younger brother of Eric Bloodaxe. The paternal line is normally more easily established than the maternal. There are a number of inexpensive paper-back guides in print which are worth reading before you start. Having acquired the rudiments of genealogy, you will need various works to help you interpret the records (which are often written in a difficult and unfamiliar hand and, before 1733, may be in Latin) and to help you find your way to the records you need.

It is a good idea to make a preliminary investigation to find out whether someone has worked on your family or is currently doing so. The Federation of Family History Societies can help; there are a number of local family history groups and one-name societies in existence and the Federation will supply a list. Enquiries should be addressed to the General Secretary. You can also consult the *National Genealogical Directory* for this purpose. There are numerous pedigrees in print and the library of the Society of Genealogists has a large collection. Many county record offices have card indexes of surnames; these can be very useful if you know roughly where your family came from.

Books

Guide to the Contents of the Public Record Office (London 1963, 1968)
K A Buckley, *Ancestry Tracing* (Birmingham, 1978)
D Iredale, *Discovering your Family Tree* (Aylesbury, 1977)
A Camp, *Everyone has Roots* (London, 1978)
E A Gooder, *Latin for Local History* (2nd edn., London, 1978)
Handbook of Dates for Students of English History, ed. C R Cheney (London, 1961)
National Genealogical Directory, ed. M J Burchall and J Warren (Brighton, 1979)
F G Emmison, *How to read Local Archives, 1500–1700* (London, 1967)
C T Martin, *The Record Interpreter* (2nd edn., London, 1910)
R E Latham, *Revised Medieval Latin Word-List* (London, 1965)
M J Kaminkov, *New Bibliography of British Genealogy* (Baltimore, 1965)
Record Repositories in Great Britain (London, 1979)
S Grimaldi, *Origines Genealogicae* (London, 1828)
R Sims, *Manual for the Genealogist* (London, 1856)
H B Guppy, *Homes of Family Names in Britain* (Baltimore, 1968)

P H Reaney, *Dictionary of British Surnames* (2nd edn., London, 1976)
C W Bardsley, *Dictionary of English and Welsh Surnames* (London, 1901)
The Surname Book and Racial History, ed S Y Gates (Salt Lake City, 1918)
P Laslett, *The World we have lost* (2nd edn., London, 1971)

II What to use in the Public Record Office

Do not start your search in the Public Record Office. Records of births, marriages and deaths, with some exceptions, are to be found elsewhere (see III/1 below). In general the genealogist has recourse to the public records for the following purposes:

to consult the Census Returns for 1841, 1851, 1861 and 1871 (see III/2 below);

to trace nonconformist (protestant or Roman Catholic) births, marriages and deaths, before 1837 (see III/1 and IV/13 and 14 below);

to trace ancestors who had or might have had some connection with the Crown or the Services (see IV/1–5, 7 below);

to find wills of (usually) wealthy ancestors who lived (usually) in the south of England or abroad, before 1858 (see III/3 below);

to find eighteenth century London marriages not recorded elsewhere (see III/1 below);

to find mentions of ancestors leaving or entering the country (see IV/15, 17 below);

to trace criminals or bankrupts (see IV/20, 21 below);

to go back beyond the period for which there are parish registers, i.e. before the sixteenth century (see V below).

A glance at the appendix and the list of contents will give you an idea of some of the questions that can be answered in the Public Record Office.

III Some useful groups of records

There are many thousands of public records and all sorts of information may be found. This handbook deals only with some of the major sources for genealogy. For a more detailed description of the Public Record Office's holdings see the published *Guide*. An updated version, the Current Guide, is available on the Reference Room shelves. *British National Archives* gives information about officially published records and printed lists and indexes.

Books

Guide to the Contents of the Public Record Office (London 1963, 1968)
British National Archives (Government Publications Sectional List 24, revised annually)

1 Births, Marriages and Deaths

a After 1837
Civil registration of births, marriages and deaths started in England and Wales in July 1837. The records are not held by the Public Record Office, but by the General Register Office, Office of Population Censuses and Surveys. Searchers are not permitted to look at the original records, and no information is available except that which is in the form of a copy certificate, which you need to purchase. A copy certificate, which takes 48 hours to prepare, can be applied for in person, if you find the reference in the indexes yourself, or by post, if you give the details of the registration you require. The certificates of births, marriages and deaths are filed separately, and reference to them is by quarterly indexes. The public search room is open from 8.30 a.m. to 4.30 p.m.

Before 1875 failure to register bore no penalty and there may be omissions in the birth registers; marriages and deaths were usually registered as this was done by the officiating clergyman or minister.

b Before 1837
The prime source for births, marriages and deaths (or rather, baptisms, marriages and burials) from the sixteenth century to 1837 is the parish register. These registers are not kept at the Public Record Office: to locate the whereabouts of one, contact the appropriate county record office, whose address will be in *Record Repositories in Great Britain*. The Society of Genealogists (see VI below) has transcripts of a large number of parish registers, and it is also in the process of

publishing a national index of them. The guide to parish registers produced in *Local Population Studies* is useful.

i Non-parochial Registers

The registers kept by nonconformist churches (i.e. those deviating from the Anglican church) are mostly in the Public Record Office (c. 9000 registers). Those that are not may be with the congregation or deposited locally. The registers in the PRO are mainly the records of protestant congregations (RG 4–RG 8). There are a few Roman Catholic registers from the north; others remain in the custody of the appropriate priest-in-charge, unless they have been deposited for safe custody with denominational, record or historical societies. Most of these registers are in the Mormon Computer File Index (see p. 7 below).

There are other registers in the PRO which may be useful sources, for example those of the British Lying-in Hospital, Holborn, which was established in 1749. It catered for the 'distressed poor (married women only) with special attention to the wives of soldiers and sailors'. There was provision both for in and out care, i.e. assistance was given with home deliveries, though most of the patients were provided with a bed in the hospital. The registers (RG 8/52–66) are in two series and run from 1749 to 1868: The 'Particulars of Patients' give the name of the patient and her husband, her parish of settlement (not her home address), date when the baby was due, date when it arrived, date of the child's baptism, its name and sex, date of the mother's admission and discharge (or death), after 1751 the mother's age and from 1755 the occupation of the father and the 'character' of the labour (normal, breech etc.). After 1812 they started giving the home address of the couple. The registers with indexes, of the nonconformist burial ground in London, at Bunhill Fields, are also in the PRO (RG 4, RG 8). The Society of Genealogists has an index to the Bunhill Fields Books of Interment, vols. 11–18 (1828–1854) in their Middlesex section; and Interment Order Books, 1789–1854, are at the Guildhall Library, as is an index of persons buried 1827–1838. The registers of the Lying-in Hospital and Bunhill Fields have been included in the Mormon Computer File Index. The registers of the former Rolls Chapel are in the PRO (PRO 30/21).

Although nonconformity started in the mid-sixteenth century, few registers pre-date 1700. Most cover the period 1775–1837. After 1754 nonconformists were obliged to marry in the local parish church so, from this date, there are usually only baptismal registers. This does not apply to Quakers and Jews (who were specifically excluded from the statute), and Roman Catholics (who largely ignored it). Nonconformist baptisms *may* be found in parochial registers of the established church following an act of 1695. Immigrants maintained their own 'foreign' churches.

It should be borne in mind that nonconformist registers often served a far wider area than did the parish church. Clues that may suggest that a search of the nonconformist registers might be fruitful are:

a family tradition;

a post 1837 marriage that took place either in a nonconformist chapel or a register office (this happened if the particular denomination did not have a registered meeting house);

if a parish register has a suspiciously high number of marriages and burials of one surname, in proportion to the number of baptisms.

As relatively few registers survive, if you have been unable to find your nonconformist ancestor, it is a good idea to look at the Court Rolls for the area (see V below). For London nonconformists between 1742 and 1840, the Dr Williams' Library Collection is very useful. There was also a central metropolitan registry for Methodists, 1818–1841. See also IV/13 below, and the Society of Genealogists *National Index*, vol. II.

ii Marriages

Until Lord Hardwicke's Marriage Act (26 Geo. II, c. 33) came into operation in 1754, marriages did not necessarily take place in the local parish church and marriages before this date may be difficult to find. Marriages are, in any case, always difficult to locate, as it was the parish church of the bride which was often chosen for the ceremony. In the eighteenth century it was fashionable to marry by licence for privacy or subterfuge. There is an article in *Family History* which gives a guide to the whereabouts of marriage licences, allegations (the affidavits sworn by the parties) and bonds, and a list of marriage indexes in *The Genealogists' Magazine*. The Boyd marriage index at the Society of Genealogists has a 12% coverage of English marriages from 1538 (see VI below).

In London, before 1754, there were a number of 'marriage shops' for ordinary folk, also patronised by the gentry. Until 1675 the popular place to marry was St James's, Duke's Place at Aldgate. From the 1620s to c. 1700 the other 'marriage church' was Holy Trinity, Minories (registers in the Guildhall Library). St Benet's, Paul's Wharf, was also popular, as it was near the Faculty Office. From 1674 until 1754 large numbers of marriages were conducted by irregular clergy in and around the Fleet Prison, and also in Mayfair, in the Mint at Southwark and in the King's Bench Prison, the records of which are in the PRO (RG 7). The Fleet Registers should be treated with extreme caution as the dates given are unreliable, and names, indeed whole entries, may be fictitious. Such clandestine marriages could result in prosecution, and there are the records of many such cases among the *ex officio* Act Books of the Commissary Court of London in the Guildhall Library. The Pallot Index, covering the years 1742–1837, contains marriages from most established churches in London, and extracts from nonconformist registers. It is held by the Institute of Heraldic and Genealogical Studies (see VI below) who will search it for a fee.

iii Divorce

Before 1858 (except in Scotland) divorce was rare and expensive, and achieved by private bill in the House of Lords. There was only one divorce bill before 1670. The church courts could decree a legal separation, known as divorce *a mensa et thoro*, but the parties had to undertake not to remarry. Alternatively the marriage could be dissolved *ab initio* on the grounds of pre-contract, a not uncommon procedure which was abolished in 1754. Records of the proceedings in the church courts, which are deposited in diocesan record offices, are largely unindexed and can be extremely difficult to interpret. Many applicants for separation went, not to their local court, but to the London Consistory Court, whose records are kept in the Greater London Record Office.

Records of divorce from 1858 to 1937 are in the PRO (J 77, J 78). The files, but not the indexes, are closed for 100 years, although permission to consult individual case papers may be obtained from the Principal Registry of the Family Division at Somerset House. For divorces since 1937, you should also apply to the Family Division.

iv Adoption

Certificates of any adoption in England and Wales since 1 January 1927 may be obtained from the Registrar General. They show the date of the adoption, the name of the child as adopted, and the full name and address of the adoptive parents. Indexes are available in St Catherine's House, and there is a separate index which links each entry with the birth register, but information from this latter index is available only to the adopted person (if over 18), to whom a copy of the birth certificate will be supplied on application to the General Register Office.

v Extra Finding Aids for Births and Deaths

One of the most useful genealogical aids now available is the Computer File Index (CFI) compiled by the Church of Jesus Christ of Latter Day Saints (Mormons). It is an index mainly of the birth entries in a large proportion of the parish registers, and some nonconformist and synagogue registers, in the British Isles. A microfiche copy can be consulted at the Hyde Park Chapel, at some other Mormon chapels, in the Guildhall Library and at the Society of Genealogists (see VI below) where you will need to book a reader. Some local record offices hold copies of those parts of the index which relate to their areas.

The records of the clearance of burial grounds, which relate to 40 cemeteries and churchyards and are deposited in the PRO (RG 37), may provide lists of the names found on monumental inscriptions. The files vary in value; some are selective, some have names but no dates, some have full transcriptions. There is a topographically arranged list but no index of names.

For births, marriages and deaths abroad and at sea, see IV/16 below.

Bibliography

Books

Abstract of Arrangements respecting Registration of Births, Marriages and Deaths (London, 1952)

'An Aid to English Research', *Family History*, vol. VII, nos. 38/39, n.s. nos. 14/15 (Aug. 1972), p. 54

K A Buckley, *Ancestry Tracing* (Birmingham, 1978)

A J Camp and L W L Edwards, 'The Computer File Index', *The Genealogists' Magazine*, vol. XIX (1978), pp. 162–163

'Marriage Licences, Bonds and Allegations', *Family History*, vol. V, no. 25, n.s. no. 1 (Jan. 1967), pp. 7–32

National Index of Parish Registers, ed. D J Steel for the Society of Genealogists (London, 1976)

'Original Parish Registers', *Local Population Studies* (1974, 1976, 1978)

M Walcot, 'English Marriage Indexes', *The Genealogists' Magazine*, vol. XIX (1978), pp. 204–208

M Walcot, 'Marriage Indexes', *Family History News and Digest*, vol. 2, no. 2 (Autumn, 1979), pp. 36–41

Published Finding Aids

Index to Local and Personal Acts, 1801–1947 (London, 1949)

Index to the Local and Personal and Private Acts, 1798–1839, ed. T Vardon (London, 1840)

List of Non-parochial Registers and Records in the Custody of the Registrar General, Main Series (List and Index Society, vol. 42)

The Registers of St Benet's, Paul's Wharf (Harleian Society, Register Section 1909–1912, which has also published many other London registers)

The Registers of St James's, Duke's Place, ed. Phillimore and Cockayne (London, 1900–1902)

Unpublished Finding Acts

Bunhill Fields Interment Order Books, 1789–1854, Guildhall Library

Boyd Marriage Index, Society of Genealogists

Index to Bunhill Fields Books of Interment, 1828–1854, Society of Genealogists (Middlesex section)

Index of Persons buried in Bunhill Fields, 1827–1838, Guildhall Library

Mormon Computer File Index, Hyde Park Chapel and Society of Genealogists

The Pallot Index to London Marriages, Institute of Heraldic and Genealogical Studies

Records

Supreme Court of Judicature

J 77   Divorce Files, 1858–1934

J 78   Indexes to Divorce Files, 1858–1885

Public Record Office

PRO 30/21   Rolls Chapel Register, 1736–1892

General Register Office

RG 4   Registers, Authenticated, 1567–1858 (includes Burial Registers of Bunhill Fields RG 4/3014–4001, indexed in 4652–4657, 1713–1838; Dr

Williams' General Register of Nonconformist baptisms, 1742–1837, RG 4/4666–4676; and the registers of the Metropolitan Wesleyan Registry, 1818–1841, RG 4/4677–4679)

RG 5   Non-parochial Certificates, 1742–1840
RG 6   Registers, Authenticated, Society of Friends, 1613–1841
RG 7   Registers, Unauthenticated, Fleet, etc., 1667–1754
RG 8   Registers, Unauthenticated, Miscellaneous, 1646–1951 (includes Burial Registers of Bunhill Fields, RG 8/35–38 and British Lying-in Hospital, Holborn, RG 8/52–66, 1749–1868)
RG 37 Removal of Graves or Tombstones, 1923–1977

2 Census Returns

The census returns of 1841, 1851, 1861 and 1871 for England and Wales (HO 107, RG 9, RG 10) are available on microfilm. In addition, a number of copies of returns are deposited locally, and a complete microfilm copy is held by the Genealogical Society of Utah. Earlier censuses were of numbers, not names. The returns are arranged topographically, and it is therefore essential to know at least the approximate address before starting a search. The information they give, from 1851 onwards, is the name, age, sex, marital status, place of birth and occupation of everyone in the house, and their relationship to the head of the household (see plate I). The 1841 Census is not as informative as the others: it does not give the relationship of the occupants to the head of the household; it states whether or not an individual was born in the county where he was living in 1841, but not his place of birth; and ages are rounded off to the nearest five years. The PRO will do a search not exceeding 5000 people for a fee, and supply the required information if found.

For a fee, the General Register Office, Office of Population Censuses and Surveys will make a search in the returns for 1881*, 1891 and 1901 to establish the age and place of birth of named persons; the exact address must be given. Such searches are made only for direct descendants or persons acting on their behalf, who should apply to the Director and Registrar General.

See also IV/9, 10 below for Irishmen and Scotsmen, and plates.

Bibliography

Books

The Census and Social Structure, an Interpretative Guide to Nineteenth Century Censuses, for England and Wales, ed. R Lawton (London, 1978)
M W Beresford, 'The unprinted Census Returns for 1841, 1851 and 1861 for England and Wales', *Amateur Historian,* V (1963), pp. 260–269

---

* Until 1982, when the 1881 returns will be available at the PRO.

J S W Gibson, *Census Returns on Microfilm, A Directory to Local Holdings* (Gulliver Press, 1979)

Records

Home Office
HO 107   Census Papers: Population Returns, 1841 and 1851

General Register Office
RG 9   1861 Census Returns
RG 10   1871 Census Returns

3 Wills and other Probate Records

Wills and related documents can be very useful to the genealogist. As well as bringing the testator to life, a will often provides a complete picture of the family, and bequests to local charities can be a clue to origins. Wills are, however, notoriously difficult to locate. It should be remembered that only a small proportion of the population made wills, and probably many of them went unproven; for an even smaller number were letters of administration taken out. Married women did not usually make wills before 1882 unless they were widowed. The mass of the working poor never went near a court of probate.

a After 1858
Wills proved from 12 January 1858 to the present day are no problem. They may be read (for a small fee) at the Principal Registry of the Family Division between 10.00 a.m. and 4.30 p.m., Monday to Friday. The same applies to letters of administration (granted if no will was made or can be found), but it is not worth paying the fee to read the original administration act book as it contains no more than does the index entry. Copies of wills are obtainable, either in person or by post, provided you know the date of death. Applications should be addressed to the Record Keeper, Correspondence Department; a handling charge is payable in addition to the copying charge. If probate was issued from a district registry, you can inspect the will there if it is more convenient than going to Somerset House. The Registry has no details of the estate other than those which appear in the will or administration. For more detailed information you can apply to the Capital Taxes Office.

b Before 1858
Before the Principal Probate Registry (now the Principal Registry of the Family Division) was set up, wills were usually proved in the church courts, of which there was a multiplicity. By and large the wills of ordinary people, where they exist, can be found in county record offices, but it may well be necessary to search through the records of several courts before any particular will is found. (See bibliography for printed guides to the whereabouts of wills.) For the period 1796–1858 the Death Duty Registers are the best means of locating a will (see page 10).

The undermentioned Houses are situate within the Boundaries of the

No. of Schedule	Road, Street, &c., and No. or Name of House	HOUSES Inhabited	HOUSES Uninhabited (U., or Building (B.)	Name and Surname of each Person	Relation to Head of Family	Condition	Age of Males	Age of Females	Rank, Profession, or Occupation	Where Born — Town of	Hamlet or Tything, &c., of	Ecclesiastical Distr. or George	Whether Blind, or Deaf-and-Dumb
	Calthorpe St			Geo. Thomson	Son	Un.	32		Architect	Astwi, Warwick			
				Anna St. Clair	Grandau	Un.		9		Birm: Do			
				Elizabeth Stokes	Serv.	Un.		26	Housemaid	Do Do			
5	33	1		Edmund Woodroof	Head	Mar.	37		Estate Agent	Cheltenham, Glos:			
				Caroline Do	Wife	Mar.		40		Amp: Loma, Surrey			
				Caroline Do	Dau	Un.		18	Scholar	Cheltenham Glos:			
				Henry Do	Son	Un.	16		Do	Birm: Warwick			
				James Do	Dau	Un.		11	Do	do			
				Laura Do	Dau	Un.		7	Do	do			
				Arthur Do	Son	Un.	6		Do	do			
				Francis Do	Son	Un.	4			do			
				Herbert Do	Son	Un.	1			do			
				Barbara Coleman	Nephew	Un.	18		Woollen Draper	Wellington, Salop:			
				Leonard Bosher	Serv.	Un.		24	Cook	Shaw, Staff:			
				Ann Stokes	Serv.	Un.		16	Housemaid?	Birm: Warwick			
6	34	1		Lucy Jackson	Serv.	Un.		18	Cook	Horsford do			
				William Edwards	Head	Mar.	67		Seed Merchant, Hay Maker	Coventry, Warwick			
				Elizabeth Do	Wife	Do		67		Birm:			
				Emma Chaffield	Niece	Un.		10	Scholar	Hillary, Wiltshire			
7	35	1		William Wilson	Head	Mar.	19		Taylor	Birm: Warwick			
				Catherine Bosher	Serv.	Mar.		83	Servant	Birm: Warwick			
				Mary Goldman	Serv.	Un.		40		Leominster H.? Wor			
8	36	1		Agnes Vener	Head	Mar.		33	Do	Edley Glos:			
				John Calvary Do	Son	Un.	39		Lace Manufacturer	Birm: Do			
				Richard Do									

I Entry in the 1861 Census for Edgbaston, Birmingham (RG 9/2124)

HIS MAJESTY'S *2ᵈ Nᵒ 73* Regiment of *Foot*
whereof *Genᵗ Lᵒᵗ George Harris* is Colonel.

THESE are to certify, that *William Robinson Rowall*
in *Capᵗ Davas* Company, in the Regiment aforesaid, born in the
Parish of *Carlisle* in or near the Town of *Carlisle*
in the County of *Cumberland* was enlisted at the Age of *Eighteen*
Years; and hath served in the said Regiment for the space of
three Years and *73*
Days, as well as in other Corps, after the Age of Eighteen, according to the following
Statement, but in consequence of *loss of left Eye from a Gun Shot*
Wound received at Waterloo on the 18ᵗʰ June 1815
is rendered unfit for further Service, and is hereby discharged; having first received
all just Demands of Pay, Clothing, &c. from his Entry into the said Regiment to
the date of this Discharge, as appears by the Receipt on the back hereof.

And to prevent any improper use being made of this Discharge, by its falling into
other Hands, the following is a Description of the said *William Robinson*
He is about *Twenty One* Years of Age; is *Five* Feet *Seven* Inches in
height, *Brown* Hair, *Grey* Eyes, *Fresh*
Complexion, by Trade a *Tailor*

STATEMENT OF SERVICE.

IN WHAT CORPS.	Period.		Serjeant Major.		Qr. Mast. Serjeant.		Serjeant.		Corporal.		Trumpeter or Drummer.		Private.		Total Service.		[included in the foregoing Total]	
	From	To	Yrs.	Days.	Yrs.	Days.	Yrs.	Days.	Yrs.	Days.	Yrs.	Days.	Yrs.	Days.	Yrs.	Days.	Years.	Days.
73ᵈ Regᵗ	7 Aprᵒ 1812	13 June 1815	..	..	..	..	..	..	..	..	..	..	3	73	3	73	2	..
TOTAL..			..	..	..	..	..	..	..	..	..	..	3	73	3	73	2	..

Given under my Hand, and Seal of the Regiment, at *Colchester*
the *13* Day of *June* 181 *8*

J Owen
Capᵗ J McConney

II Discharge document for William Robinson who lost an eye at Waterloo, 1815 (WO 97/855)

c Wills in the PRO

The PRO holds the wills proved in the senior probate court for the province of Canterbury, the Prerogative Court of Canterbury (known as the PCC). These are mainly the wills of fairly substantial people living in the south of England, although by the nineteenth century those of people of smaller means may be found in the PCC. The records cover the period 1384 to 1858, and, as many of the finding aids are not arranged in a strictly alphabetical order, a search may be a long job if the date of death is not known.

Once found, the will may be read on a microfilm of the contemporary court copy (PROB 11) of the original will, made when probate was granted. If, however, you wish to look at the original (PROB 10) for the purpose of inspecting the seal or signature, you will have to give a week's notice. Before the mid seventeenth century, the original will was often given back to the executor, so that even if you manage to find a so-called original will, it may in fact be another court copy. Beware of attaching too much importance to the seal; many testators and witnesses just took the nearest seal to hand, which often belonged to a notary's or solicitor's clerk. Relationships described in wills may not be what they seem: 'sons' may be sons-in-law, 'cousins' may be any relative, 'nieces' and 'nephews' may be grandchildren. It should also be borne in mind that a man's will did not necessarily include all the provisions he made for his children, which often involved marriage and pre-death settlements. This was particularly true of the gentry, especially in the eighteenth century, the heyday of the 'strict settlement'. Dispositions of land were not, in any case, the concern of the church courts and may therefore be omitted from pre-1858 wills. The place to look for settlements and dispositions outside the will is among private collections, and if you are lucky there may be an Estate Act of Parliament among the Local and Personal Acts.

If there is no will to be found, it may mean that letters of administration (usually abbreviated to 'admon.') issued, but do not be too sure of this. Often people did not bother to take them out unless they needed a legal title to the deceased's estate for the purpose of claiming a legacy due to the intestate, or the like. The original letters were kept by the administrator and can only be seen in private collections. What there is in the PRO is an entry in a register (PROB 6, PROB 7) giving the date of the grant, the names of the administrator and his relationship to the intestate, and, after 1796, the value of the personal estate. These valuations take no account of any real estate that the deceased might have had. Administrators were required to enter into a bond; this document may supply some extra information. Bonds certainly give the name of the person or persons who stood security with the administrator, and give some idea of the value of the estate. PCC bonds (PROB 46 and PROB 51) are not, however, available for inspection yet, but it is hoped that they will be released in batches as editorial and conservation work is finished.

There are many classes of PCC records which provide a wealth of genealogical information. Inventories of estates (see plate V) give a particularly vivid picture of the domestic scene of our ancestors, although, once again, all reference to the deceased's real estate is usually omitted (PROB 2–PROB 5, PROB 31, PROB 32,

PROB 37). Unfortunately, there is a relatively small number of PCC inventories, and, in particular, very few from before 1660 or after the end of the seventeenth century. Many were lost in the Great Fire and Interregnum, and the court ceased to call for them as a matter of course in the eighteenth century.

If an estate was subject to litigation in either the PCC or Chancery, there may be a great variety of documentation; depositions of witnesses (C 21–C 24, PROB 24, PROB 28, PROB 31, PROB 37 and PROB 47) may be especially interesting. You should first ascertain from the various indexes, or from the sentences in the will calendars (PROB 12), whether there was litigation, then look at the classes of exhibits (PROB 31, PROB 36, PROB 37), depositions and cause papers, allegations (PROB 18) and answers (PROB 25).

The Death Duty Registers (IR 26, IR 27) are very useful as a means of discovering where a will was proved or administration granted, and thus where the records now are. They also give some further information about the estate and the legatees; the address of the executor is given. Not all wills, however, are included as some estates were of insufficient value to attract tax. The registers are subject to a closure period of 125 years, but information from closed registers may be given to direct descendants or heirs, on application to the Capital Taxes Office.

For personal searchers, probate records are available in the PRO search rooms. In response to postal applications, the PRO will make a free search in the will and administration calendars, covering a period of three years from the date of death. If the search is successful, an estimate is sent to the applicant of the cost of supplying photocopies.

Wills are to be found scattered throughout the public records. Among the papers of the Bona Vacantia division of the Treasury Solicitor's Office (TS 17) there are records relating to intestates' estates which escheated to the Crown, there being no next of kin, a common fate for the personal estates of unmarried bastards. There are a number of pedigrees among these papers.

For wills of Irishmen and Scots see IV/9, 10 below.

Bibliography

Books

A J Camp, *Wills and their Whereabouts* (4th edn., London, 1974)

English Probate Jurisdictions, leaflets with maps (Genealogical Society of the Church of Jesus Christ of Latter Day Saints)
J S W Gibson, *Wills and where to find them* (London, 1974)
The Records of the Prerogative Court of Canterbury (PRO Provisional Guide, revised ed., 1979)

Published Finding Aids

Administrations in the Prerogative Court of Canterbury, 1559–1571, 1572–1580, ed. R M Glencross (Exeter, 1912, 1917), *1620–1630,* ed. J H Morrison (London, 1935)

Administrations in the Prerogative Court of Canterbury, 1581–1595, ed. C H Ridge (1954), *1596–1608, 1609–1619,* ed. M Fitch (1964–1968), *1649–1654,* ed. J Ainsworth (1944), *1655–1660,* ed. C H Ridge (1949–1953), (London, British Record Society, Index Library)

PCC Will Index, 1750–1800, vol. 1, *A–Bh* (1976), vol. II, *Bi–Ce* (1977), ed. A J Camp (London, Society of Genealogists)

P W Coldham, *English Estates of American Colonists* (Baltimore, 1980) (PCC Wills and Admons., 1700–1799)

Prerogative Court of Canterbury Sentences, 1630–1639, ed. J and G F Matthews (London, 1907)

Prerogative Court of Canterbury Wills, vols. I and II, *1383–1558,* ed. J C C Smith (1893–1895), vol. III, *1558–1583,* ed. S A Smith and L L Duncan (1898), vol. IV, *1584–1604,* ed. S A Smith and E A Fry (1901), vol. V, *1605–1619,* ed. E Stokes (1912), vol. VI, *1620–1629,* vol. VII, *1653–1656,* ed. R H E Hill (1912, 1925), vol. VIII, *1657–1660,* ed. T M Blagg (1936), vol. IX, *1671–1675,* ed. J Ainsworth (1942), vol. X, *1676–1685,* vol. XI, *1686–1693,* ed. C H Ridge, (1948, 1955–1956), vol. XII, *1694–1700,* ed. M Fitch (1959–1960), (London, British Record Society, Index Library)

Probate Acts in the Prerogative Court of Canterbury, vol. I, *1630–1639* (1903), vol. II, *1640–1644* (1905), vol. III, *1645–1647* (1906), vol. IV, *1648–1649* (1906), vol. V, *1650–1651* (1909), vol. VI, *1652–1653* (1911), ed. J and G F Matthews (London)

Wills in the Public Record Office (Baltimore, 1968)

Unpublished Finding Aids

Card indexes of estates litigated in the PCC, 1666–1713 and PCC pleadings, 1661–c.1800

Card index of PCC Wills 1721–1725, Society of Genealogists

Indexes to Cause Papers (PROB 28 and PROB 37)

Indexes to disputed estates in Chancery, *1575–1714,* compiled by P W Coldham, MS, by name of deceased

Indexes to PCC Exhibits, 1722–1858, photo-copy (PROB 33)

Indexes to PCC Wills, 1700–1858, MS (PROB 12)

Lists of Inventories, TS (card indexes available on request)

Records

Chancery

C 21	Depositions taken by Commission (Country Depositions), Elizabeth I to Charles I
C 22	Country Depositions, 1649–1714
C 23	Sealed Depositions, Elizabeth I to Victoria
C 24	Town Depositions, 26 Henry VIII to 1853

Inland Revenue Office
IR 26   Estate Duty Office, Death Duty Registers, from 1796*
IR 27   Indexes to Death Duty Registers, 1796–1903

Prerogative Court of Canterbury
PROB 2   Inventories, 1464–1660
PROB 3   Inventories, 1718–1782
PROB 4   Parchment Inventories, 1661–1720 (card index available)
PROB 5   Paper Inventories, 1661–1732
PROB 6   Administration Act Books, 1559–1858
PROB 8   Probate Act Books, 1526–1858
PROB 10   Original Wills, 1383–1858
PROB 11   Registered Copy Wills, 1383–1858
PROB 12   Register Books (Calendars of Wills), 1383–1858
PROB 18   Allegations, 1661–1858
PROB 24   Depositions, 1657–1809
PROB 25   Answers, 1664–1854
PROB 26   Depositions, bound by Suit, 1826–1857
PROB 28   Cause Papers, 1642–1722
PROB 31   Exhibits, 1722–1858 (indexes in PROB 33, and index of inventories, available on request)
PROB 32   Filed exhibits with Inventories, c. 1661–c. 1700†
PROB 33   Indexes to exhibits, 1683–1858 (PROB 31, PROB 37)
PROB 36   Exhibits, 1653–1721† (card index available on request)
PROB 37   Cause Papers, 1783–1858
PROB 46   Administration Bonds†
PROB 47   Proctors' Case Papers†
PROB 51   Adminstration Bonds, Sixteenth Century*

Treasury Solicitor
TS 17   Bona Vacantia Division: Papers, 1808–1964

4 Records of Change of Name

From the late nineteenth century deeds poll were often, although not always, enrolled, and these enrolments may be seen at the PRO (C 54, J 18). Since 1914, all enrolled deeds poll have been published in the London Gazette, but for changes of name in the last three years, apply to Room 81, Royal Courts of Justice. For deeds poll that were not enrolled, look in the local and national press, and if all else fails your family solicitor may be able to help.

Bibliography

Published Finding Aids

An Index to Change of Names, 1760–1901, ed. W P W Phillimore and E A Fry (London, 1905)
London Gazette (1665 to date)

---

* There are Registers to 1894 but they are closed for 125 years.
† These classes are not yet available.

5 Apprenticeship Records

The training of working men was not usually recorded and indentures of apprenticeship were private documents. If they survive at all they will normally be in private hands; there is a small collection at the Society of Genealogists. Between 1710 and 1811, however, apprenticeship indentures were subject to tax and the records relating to this tax are in the PRO (IR 1, Indexes in IR 17). Duty was payable by the master at the rate of 6*d.* for every £1 under £50 which he received for taking on the apprentice, and 1*s.* for every £1 above that sum. The deadline for payment was one year after the expiry of the indenture; it may therefore be necessary to search the records of several years' payments in order to find a particular entry, even when the date of the indenture is known.

The Apprenticeship Books record the names, addresses and trades of the masters, the names of the apprentices and dates of their indentures. Until 1752 the names of apprentices' parents are given, but after that year, rarely. There are indexes of masters' names from 1710 to 1762, and of apprentices' names from 1710 to 1774. These were made on behalf of the Society of Genealogists and copied from the originals in the Guildhall Library, London. Further indexes, for later dates, are in preparation.

Where the stamp duty was paid in London, entries will be found in the 'City' registers in this series; where it was paid elsewhere, entries will be found in the 'Country' registers.

It is important to note that masters did not have to pay stamp duty for apprentices taken on at the common or public charge of any township or parish, or by or out of any public charity (8 Anne, c. 5, s. 50). This means that very many apprentices were never subject to the duty, and are therefore not mentioned in the registers. In such cases, local or charity records, if they survive, are likely to be the only source of information on individuals. London Livery Companies keep full records of membership, which give places of birth, previous residences and other details. For these, apply to the Guildhall Library. Among the War Office records there is a list of apprentices who enlisted in the Army but had to return to their masters until their indentures expired, 1806 to 1835 (WO 25/2962).

a Naval Apprentices
Information about dockyard workers and other naval apprentices may be found among the Admiralty and Navy Board Correspondence (ADM 1, ADM 106). You

should look under the headings 'Boys' (code 13) and 'Apprentices in Dockyards' (code 41.16) in the Admiralty Digest (ADM 12). There are Apprenticeship Registers for Greenwich Hospital for the years 1808 to 1838 (ADM 73/421, 448). Marks and results of examinations for dockyard and artificer apprentices from 1876 are to be found among the records of the Civil Service Commission (CSC 10).

b Merchant Naval Apprentices
There are indexes of apprentices registered in the Merchant Service between 1824 and 1953 (BT 150). The earlier volumes give name, date and terms of indenture and the name of the master. Entries in later volumes include the port where the apprentice signed on and the ship's name.

Bibliography

Books

W B Stephens, *Sources of English Local History* (Manchester, 1973)

Published Finding Aids

Alphabetical Guide to War Office and Other Material, PRO Lists and Indexes, vol. LIII.

Records

Admiralty
ADM 1   Admiralty and Secretariat Papers, 1660–1969
ADM 12   Admiralty and Secretariat Indexes and Compilations, Series III,
          1660–1938
ADM 73/421, 448   Greenwich Hospital Registers, Boys Apprenticed, Lower
                  School, 1808–1838; Girls Apprenticed, 1808–1837
ADM 106   Navy Board Records, 1659–1837
Registrar General of Shipping and Seamen
BT 150   Index of Apprentices, 1824–1953
Civil Service Commission
CSC 10   Examination, Tables of Marks and Results, 1876–1959
Inland Revenue Office
IR 1   Apprenticeship Books, 1710–1811
IR 17   Indexes to Apprenticeship Books, 1710–1774
War Office
WO 25/2962   Recruits claimed as apprentices, 1806–1835

6 Tax Records

Tax records in the PRO of most use to the genealogist are the Hearth Tax returns and assessments of 1662–1674. These relate to the levy of two shillings on every hearth and are found in the class of Lay Subsidies (E 179). The class also contains a number of earlier tax returns and assessments, but few of these include lists of names; where they do, the fact is noted in the class list. The most complete Hearth Tax records are those for 25 March 1664. Information supplied includes names of householders, sometimes their status, and the number of hearths for which they were chargeable. The number of hearths is a clue to wealth and status. Over seven hearths usually indicates gentry and above; between four and seven hearths are wealthy craftsmen and tradesmen, merchants and yeomen; between two and three are most craftsmen, tradesmen and yeomen; the labouring poor, husbandmen and poor craftsmen usually only had one hearth. There are many gaps in the records, partly because of the loss of documentation, but partly also owing to widespread evasion of this most unpopular tax. The indexes in the PRO are arranged topographically. Hearth Tax returns for particular areas have been published by many local record societies (see card index of records in print), and some records are to be found in county record offices, among the quarter sessions records.

Land Tax assessments may be found in county record offices for the period 1780–1832. In the PRO are the Land Tax Redemption Office Quotas and Assessments (IR 23). They list all owners of property subject to Land Tax in England and Wales in 1798–1799. The arrangement is by Land Tax parish and there is no index of names.

The Land Revenue Commission Field Books (IR 58) give the names of all freeholders and details of the property they held from 1910 to 1913. The arrangement is topographical and the means of reference, which are the maps, are kept at present in the District Valuation Offices, and in many cases also in county record offices. You should look at these maps before visiting the PRO.

Bibliography

Books

L M Marshall, 'The Levying of the Hearth Tax 1662–1668', *English Historical Review*, vol. 51 (1936), pp. 628–646
C A F Meekings, *Introduction to The Survey Hearth Tax, 1664*, Surrey Record Society 17 (1940)

Unpublished Finding Aids

PRO card index of records in print
List of Exchequer K R Subsidy Rolls etc., Lay Series, vols. I–IX (topographical arrangement, TS)

Records

Exchequer: The King's Remembrancer
E 179   Subsidy Rolls, c. Henry II to William and Mary

Inland Revenue Office
IR 23   Land Tax Redemption Office, Quotas and Assessments, 1798–1801, 1828–1914
IR 58   Valuation Office, Field Books, 1910–1913

7 Deeds and other Records of Landownership

In England, records of landownership and transfer are difficult to locate. There was no legal requirement to keep deeds, and no system of registration before the nineteenth century, except in Middlesex, Yorkshire and some cities. The Middlesex register is available for search in the Greater London Council Record Office. For Yorkshire deeds apply to the record office of the appropriate riding. The majority of ordinary people held land by a form of tenure called copyhold, abolished in 1925. The record of the copyhold was an entry on the roll of the local manor court. To trace the whereabouts of Court Rolls, apply to the Manorial Register, Historical Manuscripts Commission. In most cases it is probably best to make the first approach to the county record office or local archaeological society. National registration of land started (with London) in the early nineteenth century. Land in all the major conurbations is now registered, but there are still some rural areas where registration is not compulsory. For information from the registers apply to HM Land Registry. You will need the permission of the present occupant before any details can be given to you.

There are many thousands of deeds in the PRO, but there is no general index and a speculative search is not advised: some private conveyances were enrolled; private deeds came into the possession of the Crown when land was acquired; and deeds could be produced as exhibits in law suits. The records are scattered over a large number of classes. Trust deeds (deeds relating to grants of land for charitable purposes) were enrolled on the Close Rolls of the Chancery (C 54) from 1735 until 1925. The largest collections of deeds in the PRO are probably the conveyances on the Recovery Rolls (CP 43), the Plea Rolls of the Court of Common Pleas (CP 40) and the Close Rolls. There are also documents known as Feet of Fines (CP 25). These are the records of fictitious law suits, entered into in order to avoid regulations restricting conveyance of land. The intended purchaser as plaintiff, claimed the property from the vendor. The means of reference to the Plea and Recovery Rolls are difficult to handle; they are contemporary manuscript calendars (which are hard to read) in chronological order with the name of the county in the margin. There are no indexes of names. For the Feet of Fines there are similar indexes, but many of the fines have been printed and indexed by local record societies. The indexes to the deeds on the Close Rolls (sixteenth to nineteenth century) are much more easily usable; they are arranged by the names of the grantee and grantor. It should be borne in mind that land transactions in the Palatinates of Chester (CHES), Durham (DURH), and Lancaster (PL) were enrolled (if at all) on the rolls of the local courts, and should be sought among the records of these palatinates. There are some deeds of the Augmentation Office (E 326–E 330), which relate to land which came under the cognizance of the Exchequer following the dissolution of the monasteries, and there is a series of Exchequer (T.R.) deeds which runs from the twelfth century (E 40–E 44). There are also lists of copyholders who converted to freehold, a practice which started in the 1840s and was made compulsory by the Law of Property Acts, 1922, 1924 (MAF 9, MAF 13, MAF 27). The lists are arranged by county with the names of the copyholders given under the relevant manor.

Bibliography

Books

A A Dibben, *Title Deeds* (Historical Association, Helps for Students of History, no. 72, 1968)
J H Harvey, *Sources for the History of Houses* (British Records Association, Archives and the User, no. 3, 1974)

Published Finding Aids

Catalogue of Ancient Deeds, before c. 1603 (London, 1890–1915)
Exchequer, Augmentation Office, Ancient Deeds Series B (*E 326/4233–12950*), calendar and index (List and Index Society, vols. 95, 101, 113, 124), and *Series BB* (*E 328*), list and index (List and Index Society, vol. 137)
Exchequer (T.R.), *Ancient Deeds Series A* (*E 40/13673–15910*), descriptive list (List and Index Society, vols. 151, 152)

Unpublished Finding Aids

Catalogue of Lists and Indexes, King's Bench and Common Pleas, TS (for indexes to Plea and Recovery Rolls)
Indexes to the Close Rolls, MS
Lists and indexes of Ancient Deeds, TS
Lists of copyhold land converted to freehold, MAF 9, MAF 13, MAF 27, TS
Private conveyances in the PRO, PRO leaflet no. 25
PRO card index of records in print

Records

Chancery
C 54   Close Rolls, 6 John to 1903

Court of Common Pleas
CP 25   Feet of Fines, Henry II to 2 Victoria
CP 40   Plea Rolls, 1 Edward I to 38 Victoria (indexes in IND 1–6605)
CP 43   Recovery Rolls, 25 Elizabeth I to 1837 (indexes in IND 16943–9, 17183–17216)

Palatinate of Chester
CHES 2   Enrolments, 1 Edward II to 11 George IV
CHES 31   Fines and Recoveries, 9 Edward I to 1 William IV
CHES 32   Enrolments of Fines and Recoveries, 28 Elizabeth I to Anne

Palatinate of Durham
DURH 12   Feet of Fines, 1535–1834
DURH 21   Deeds, Series G, 17th Century

Exchequer: Treasury of Receipt
E 40   Ancient Deeds (12th Century to 1603), Series A
E 41   Ancient Deeds, Series AA
E 42   Ancient Deeds, Series AS
E 43   Ancient Deeds, Series WS
E 44   Modern Deeds, 17th Century

Exchequer: Augmentations Office
E 326   Ancient Deeds (to the end of Elizabeth I), Series B
E 327   Ancient Deeds, Series BX
E 328   Ancient Deeds, Series BB
E 329   Ancient Deeds, Series BS
E 330   Modern Deeds, from James I

Ministry of Agriculture, Fisheries and Food
MAF 9   Deeds and Awards of Enfranchisement, 1841–1925
MAF 13   Extinguishment of Manorial Incidents, 1926–1944
MAF 27   Certificates of Determination of Compensation under the Law of
             Property Acts (1922, 1924), 1937–1957

Palatinate of Lancaster
PL 2   Close Rolls, Henry IV, Henry VI, Edward IV
PL 14   Miscellanea, Richard II to Victoria
PL 15   Plea Rolls, 2 Henry IV to 11 Victoria
PL 17   Fines, 1362 to 4 William IV
PL 29   Deeds, Series H, 16th to 19th Century

Principality of Wales
WALE 29   Ancient Deeds, Series F, Edward I to Elizabeth I
WALE 30   Ancient Deeds, Series FF, Elizabeth I
WALE 31   Modern Deeds, from James I

8 Legal Proceedings

The PRO holds records of all the central law courts, including the records of assize circuits (ASSI). The records of some of the county courts (AK) are also there, beginning in the 1840s. Records of quarter sessions are held locally; many have been calendared and are in print. If you are embarking on a hunt for anything you can find about your ancestors, without definite information about any specific suit, it is probably best to start with quarter sessions records.

By and large the records of the central courts of common law are best avoided; they are difficult to read and understand, and not particularly fruitful. Means of reference, where they exist, may be complicated. If searching for a specific case, you must know the name of the plaintiff, the date, and the court where the action took place. For the nineteenth century you will invariably find reports printed in newspapers much more informative than the extant documentation. For Sussex, Surrey, Kent, Essex and Hertfordshire there are printed calendars of assize records, for the reigns of Elizabeth I and James I. They are fully indexed and well worth looking at.

The records of the courts of equity, which begin in the late fourteenth century and continue to the nineteenth, are easier to use and more informative than those of the common law courts. There were nine courts: Chancery (C), which handled the most business; Exchequer (E); Star Chamber (STAC) and the Court of Requests (REQ), both of which existed only from the late fifteenth to the mid seventeenth century; the Court of the Duchy of Lancaster (DL); the Palatinate

Courts of Lancaster (PL), Chester (CHES) and Durham (DURH); and the Court of Augmentations (E), for former monastic land only. From 1873 the Chancery Division of the Supreme Court of Judicature took over all equity jurisdiction. The equity courts had written proceedings in English. They competed for business with one another, dealing with disputes over land, wills, marriage settlements, etc. There are various means of reference available in the PRO. They are mostly manuscript indexes by the name of the plaintiffs (surnames only). Because of the huge volume of business handled in Chancery, and the arrangement of the records, the search for individuals may be a protracted procedure. It is a good idea to use the microfilm of the Bernau index at the Society of Genealogists for the eighteenth century; this contains references to every Chancery litigant between 1714 and 1758, and also includes all Exchequer deponents from 1559 to 1695. There are various lists, indexes and calendars of Chancery Proceedings from the reign of Richard II to the seventeenth century. From the reign of James I until 1842 Chancery Proceedings are arranged in six concurrent series. If there is no printed or microfilm index for the period you are searching, because of this division into the Six Clerks Series you should go to the indexes to the Decree and Order Books (1544–1875). Having followed the account of the case through the Decree and Order Books you can then, if necessary, look for other proceedings: bills, answers, etc.

Disputes concerning ships or cargoes were heard in the Admiralty Court (HCA). The records of this court are not easy to use but can be very informative if a relevant case is located.

a Unclaimed Money (Dormant Funds)
These are cash and securities under the control of the Supreme Court in accounts which have not been dealt with for upwards of fifteen years (England only). Searches can be made free of charge in the 1922–1952 list in the Eastern Corridor, Ground Floor, Royal Courts of Justice. Enquiries should be sent to the Chief Accountant, Supreme Court Pay Office, Royal Courts of Justice; evidence of beneficial interest is required. Lists of funds, published as supplements to the London Gazette (1893–1974), can be consulted in the PRO.

b Pedigrees
Pedigrees were frequently produced as evidence in law suits but, except in a few classes, it is very difficult to find them. For the eighteenth and nineteenth centuries there are manuscript indexes of pedigrees in some classes of Chancery Masters Exhibits (C 103–C 114) on the open shelves. Most of these pedigrees relate to disputed wills and administrations. A TS index to pedigrees among various Supreme Court papers is in preparation.

For criminal proceedings see IV/21 below.

Bibliography

Books

R E F Garrett, *Chancery and other Legal Proceedings* (Shalfleet Manor, 1968)
An Introduction to Chancery Proceedings, PRO Leaflet No. 32

Published Finding Aids

Calendar of Assize Records, Hertfordshire Indictments, Elizabeth I and *James I*, ed.
J S Cockburn (London, 1975)
Calendar of Assize Records, Sussex Indictments, Elizabeth I and *James I*, ed. J S
Cockburn (London, 1975)
Calendar of Assize Records, Essex Indictments, Elizabeth I and *James I*, ed. J S
Cockburn (London, 1978 and 1981)
Calendar of Assize Records, Kent Indictments, Elizabeth I and *James I*, ed. J S
Cockburn (London, 1979 and 1981)
Calendar of Assize Records, Surrey Indictments, Elizabeth I and *James I*, ed. J S
Cockburn (London, 1980 and 1981)
Calendar of Proceedings in Chancery in the Reign of Queen Elizabeth I ed. J
Caley and J Bayley (London, Record Commission, 1827–1832)
Calendar of Chancery Proceedings, Bills and Answers filed in the reign of Charles I,
vols. 1–3, ed. W P W Phillimore, vol. 4, ed. E A Fry (British Records Society,
Index Library, 1903–1904)
Index Nominum of Early Chancery Proceedings, 1386–1467, ed. C A Walmisley
(Harleian Society, vols. LXXVIII–LXXIX, 1927–1928)
Index of Chancery Proceedings, PRO Lists and Indexes, vol. VII, *1558–1579*
(1896), vol. XXIV, *1579–1621* (1908), vol. XXX, *1621–1660* (1909)
Index of Chancery Proceedings, James I, A–K only, PRO Lists and Indexes, vol.
XLVII (1922)
Index of Chancery Proceedings, 1603–1625, A–L only, ed. R Topham, *The
Genealogist*, n.s. vols. IV, VI–IX (1887, 1889–1892)
Index of Chancery Proceedings, Bridges' Division, 1613–1714, PRO Lists and
Indexes, vol. XXXIX (1913), vol. XLII (1914), vol. XLIV (1915), vol. XLV (1917)
Index of Chancery Proceedings, Reynardson's Division, 1649–1714, ed. E A Fry
(British Records Society, Index Library, 1903–1904)
Lists of Early Chancery Proceedings, PRO Lists and Indexes, vol. XII, *9 Ric.
II–Edw. IV* (1901), vol. XVI, *1467–1485* (1903), vol. XX, *1485–1500* (1906),
vol. XXIX, *1500–1515* (1908), vol. XXXVIII, *1515–1529* (1912), vol. XLVIII,
1529–1538 (1922), vol. L, *1533–1538* (1927), vol. LI, *1538–1544* (1929), vol.
LIV, *1544–1553* (1933), vol. LV, *1553–1558* (1936)
*List and Index to the Proceedings in the Star Chamber for the Reign of James I
(1603–1625) in the PRO*, ed. T G Barnes (Chicago, 1975)
Indexes to Proceedings in the Court of Requests, Henry VII to James I, PRO Lists
and Indexes, Supplementary, vol. VII (New York, 1964–1974)

Unpublished Finding Aids

Index of Chancery Proceedings, ed. C Bernau, for PRO classes C 11, C 12, C 21,
C 24, 8% of C 22 and parts of Exchequer (microfilm at the Society of
Genealogists)
Index of Chancery Proceedings, James I, L–Z only, MS
Indexes to disputed estates in Chancery, Collins Division, Hamilton Division,
Mitford Division, Whittington Division, 1649–1714, ed. P W Coldham, arranged
by name of deceased

Indexes of Chancery Proceedings, 1714–1758, 1758–1800, 1800–1842, MS and TS

Index of Chancery Affidavits from 1615 (C 31, C 41), PRO IND 14545 *et seq.*

Index of Supreme Court Pedigrees (J 46, J 63, J 64), TS

Index of Town Depositions, Henry VIII to Mary (C 24), Deponents, IND 16759, Depositions, IND 9115–9121

Index of Country Depositions, 1649–1714 (C 11, C 12, C 21, C 22), topographical index 1714–1744, TS and MS at Society of Genealogists

Index of Decrees and Orders, 1544–1841 (C 33), IND 1388 *et seq.*

Index of Reports and Certificates, 1606–1759 (C 38), IND 1878–2028; 1760–1800 IND 10700; 1800–1841, IND 14919–14959

Index of Exchequer Deponents, 1559–1695, TS

Various indexes to Star Chamber records, 1485–James I, MS

List and index of Supreme Court Central Office documents exhibited, 19th–20th century (J 90), TS

Records

ASSI	Clerks of Assize
AK	County Courts
C	Chancery
C 103–C 114	Masters' Exhibits, 13th to 19th century
CHES	Palatinate of Chester
DURH	Palatinate of Durham
DL	Duchy of Lancaster
E	Exchequer
HCA	High Court of Admiralty
J	Supreme Court of Judicature
PL	Palatinate of Lancaster
REQ	Court of Requests
STAC	Court of Star Chamber

9 Tontines and Annuity Records

Tontines were government money raising schemes, of which there were eleven between 1693 and 1789. In return for an original investment participants were guaranteed a yearly income for the life of a living nominee chosen by the investor. People usually nominated their youngest relative. As the nominees died off, the central fund was distributed between fewer and fewer people and the annuity therefore became more valuable as the years passed. There were in all about 15,000 participants. The records (NDO 1–NDO 3) may give details concerning the marriages, deaths, and wills of contributors and nominees. Contributors were usually quite substantial people and many of them came from the south of England. Many were spinsters. The registers have integral indexes.

The records of the Irish Tontine are particularly useful because of the general dearth of Irish material (NDO 3).

Bibliography

F Leeson, *A Guide to the Records of the British State Tontines and Life Annuities of the 17th and 18th Centuries* (Shalfleet Manor, 1968)

Records

National Debt Office
NDO 1   Life Annuities (1745–1757) and Tontine (1789), 1745–1843
NDO 2   Life Annuities (1766–1779) and Tontine (1789), 1776–1888
NDO 3   Irish Tontines (1773–1777), 1773–1871

10 Tithe Records

Tithes (the tax of a tenth of all produce, payable to the local clergyman) were a source of dispute over the years. In 1836 the Tithe Commutation Act was passed and a fixed money payment was substituted. The records emanating from this procedure, in the form of maps and apportionments, copies of which are held in county record offices as well as at the PRO (IR 29, IR 30), supply names of landowners and occupiers for a large number of parishes and chapelries, with details of the holdings and a description of the state of cultivation. There were many areas where tithes had already been commuted for land or money in the course of private enclosures. For these areas there are, of course, no records in the Inland Revenue classes. Also, there were a good many districts in which, although the tithes were commuted under the provisions of the 1836 Act, no apportionment was made. This was either because the amount involved was negligible or because the landowners were themselves the tithe owners, and the agreement or award of a gross tithe rentcharge was followed by the redemption or merger of the tithe rentcharges. By this means the expense of a formal apportionment and of the preparation of a map was avoided. In such cases the result of the proceedings will be recorded in a formal agreement or instrument of merger (TITH 3), and there should be a Tithe file (IR 18) which is often informative.

Bibliography

Published Finding Aids

Lists of Inland Revenue Tithe Maps and Apportionments, vol. I, *Bedford to Northumberland*; vol. II *Nottingham to Yorkshire, Wales* (List and Index Society vols. 68 and 83)

Records

Inland Revenue Office
IR 18   Tithe Files 1836–c. 1870
IR 29   Tithe Redemption Office: Tithe Apportionments, 19th Century
IR 30   Tithe Redemption Office: Tithe Maps, 19th Century

Tithe Redemption Commission
TITH 1   Boundary Awards, 1839–1842, 1860
TITH 2   Sealed Originals, 1836–1866
TITH 3   Declarations of Merger, 1837–1936

IV Special groups of people

1 Soldiers

If a census return, parish register or family tradition tells you that your ancestor was a soldier, it may well be worth your while looking for his service record in the PRO. Some of these records may give information about families, domiciles and even physical descriptions. You may be started on the trail by finding out that your ancestor was a Chelsea or Kilmainham pensioner, which means he was in receipt of an army pension.

Service records of the British Army are in the PRO. There are few from before 1660, the main collection at present covering the years 1660–1900. The records 1900–1913 are still in the process of being transferred. For the period since 1913 for other ranks you should make a written application to the Army Records Centre; the records of officers' services until 1954 are at the PRO, except for the Royal Artillery who have their own record office. For information about pensions of men injured in the First World War, and for relatives of those killed in action, see the records of the Paymaster General (PMG) or write to the Department of Health and Social Security in Nelson; casualty lists for the war have been published, and copies are available in the British Library or by appointment at the Imperial War Museum.

For the Second World War, the most useful sources in the PRO are the War Diaries (WO 165–WO 179) arranged by unit. You will need to sign an undertaking of confidentiality before looking at the War Diaries.

There was no regular standing army in Britain before the Civil War (1642–1649). Regiments were raised to meet special requirements and were usually known by the names of the colonels who raised them. Such references as there are to individual soldiers should be sought among the State Papers Domestic (SP), State Papers Foreign (SP) and the Exchequer and Audit Office Accounts (AO 1–AO 3). It would be unusual to find any reference in these sources to birthplace, wife or family of an individual. Other places to look might be Exchequer Issues (E 403) and Exchequer Accounts (E 101) for the payment of military wages, the State Papers (SP) for widows' pensions, the Licences to pass beyond the Seas (E 157), for oaths of allegiance taken by soldiers going to the Low Countries in 1613 to 1624, and the Commonwealth Exchequer Papers for the army during the Interregnum (SP 28).

a Organisation

Some basic grasp of the organisation of the army is necessary for the proper use of military records. The army was divided into commissioned officers, recruited from the top level of society, as they were the people who could afford to buy commissions; and other ranks, the lowest of whom were often drawn from the poorest classes, including criminals and paupers. Between 1780 and 1914 there was voluntary enlistment, normally for life. Whenever a new regiment was needed a colonel was given a 'beating order' to enlist, and recruitment headquarters were established, usually in local inns. Few soldiers stayed the course for the whole of their life: some bought themselves out; some were wounded, incapacitated and discharged; many were discharged at the end of the various wars. Boys had to be eighteen before they could be legally enlisted, but this rule was not always observed. Garrisons were established for the quartering of troops throughout the country, and in times of stress when the garrison troops were needed elsewhere, special battalions of veterans would be raised to take their place. The basic unit of the army was the regiment, under the command of a colonel, usually consisting of several companies (or, in the cavalry, troops) of about a hundred men each. These regiments were of various types: cavalry (on horseback), infantry (foot soldiers), artillery (to fire the cannons) and engineers (to construct bridges, roads and mines).

There was an army in India for many years, maintained by the East India Company, which only became part of the British Army proper in 1859. For records relating to soldiers in India before this date, you should apply to the India Office Library.

b Officers

There were four sorts of officer:

general officers, who co-ordinated the efforts of the whole army: field marshal, general, lieutenant general, major general.

regimental officers: colonel (in command of a regiment), lieutenant colonel, major.

company officers: captain (in command of a company), and his subalterns: lieutenant and cornet (cavalry) or ensign (infantry). Cornets and ensigns became second lieutenants in 1871.

others: paymaster, adjutant (an administrative assistant), quartermaster (in charge of accommodation and stores), surgeon, chaplain.

Officers should be easy to find. First look in the *Army Lists*, which begin in 1754 and are available in good libraries. There is also a manuscript regimental list for 1702 to 1823 (WO 64). For family details you could look among the applications for commissions in Commander in Chief's Memoranda (WO 31) from 1793, and in the widows' pension applications (WO 42).

Before 1829 there is no certainty of finding what you are looking for. After that date it is more likely as systematic records began to be kept. These are arranged by regiment, but some regiments' records have not been transferred to the PRO and are presumed lost. Having found your officer in the *Army List*, your next step is to consult the War Office Registers (WO 25) which contain, among other things, a series of returns of officers' services, the most useful being those for 1808–1810 (no personal details), 1829 to 1919 (officers on active service) and 1829 (retired officers). These registers are supplemented by the Records of Officers' Services, c. 1771–1954 (WO 76). There are some baptismal, marriage and death certificates for 1755 to 1908 (WO 42), and also the date of an officer's death can usually be found in the Paymaster General's Records of Full and Half Pay (PMG 3, PMG 4). As a last resort, the *Gentleman's Magazine* may be helpful. The Royal Military Academy, Sandhurst, will supply details of cadets.

c Other Ranks

The enlisted men were privates (troopers in the cavalry), trumpeters and drummers, supervised by corporals and sergeants, non-commissioned officers promoted from the ranks.

To find records relating to an ordinary soldier who was discharged to pension before 1883, unless you are prepared for a very long search indeed, you must know the name of the regiment or a campaign he fought in. Regimental names usually appear on census returns (see III/2 above), probate records (III/3 above) and Chaplains' returns (IV/16 below). After 1883 this is not necessary as the discharge papers are arranged alphabetically through the entire army. The Regular Soldiers Documents (WO 97) (see plate V) are the main series of service records and contain the details of a soldier's army service until he was discharged to pension. They cover the period 1756 to 1913, although the last thirteen years are still in the process of being transferred from the Army Records Centre, and, after 1883, contain some family details as well as personal information. You may also find something in the Medal Rolls (WO 100) if you know your ancestor fought in a particular campaign.

The records of soldiers who died in the service have not survived, so, for such men you will have to look in the Muster Books and Pay Lists (WO 10, WO 13, WO 16), which may be a lengthy task as not only are they arranged regimentally, but also each volume covers only a twelve month period. In many of these volumes, you will find a form showing 'Men becoming non-effective' at the end of each quarter. Where this exists, it should show the birthplace of the man discharged or dead, his trade and his date of enlistment. By tracing him back through the Muster Books it may be possible to find his age shown on the day of enlistment as a recruit. The Musters also contain Marriage Rolls after about 1868, which sometimes include information about children as well as wives (and see IV/16 below). The entry of a recruit in the Musters generally gives his age and the place he joined but does not give his birthplace. When the unit in which a man served is not known, but a place and date are given, you can find out which regiments were stationed there from the Monthly Returns (WO 17, WO 73). The Musters of regimental depots are usually bound in with the other musters of regiments based at home until about 1872.

i South African (Boer) War, 1899–1902
The service documents of British regular soldiers who served in South Africa were, for the most part, destroyed by enemy bombing in the Second World War. Those which survived are in the process of being transferred from the Army Records Centre to the PRO. The Medal Rolls (WO 100) sometimes contain a few personal details, such as the date of discharge or death, and the home address. For the British Auxiliary Forces, you will find some records of the City Imperial Volunteers at the Guildhall Library, and the soldiers' documents of the Imperial Yeomanry are at the PRO (WO 128). You will also find enrolment forms and nominal rolls of local armed forces (WO 126, WO 127), and enlistment papers and rolls of those who took part in the campaign (WO 108).

ii American War of Independence, 1776–1783
The Muster Books and Pay Lists of many regiments that took part in this war may be found, but the discharge certificates of men discharged in North America, which give the age and place of birth, can very seldom be traced. It is unlikely that you will find anything but a man's name, rank and date of discharge in the musters. There are some pay lists and account books for Hessian troops, but they provide few personal details; some Audit Office accounts (AO 3) may be useful. The Loyalist Regiment Rolls for provincial troops are in the Public Archives of Canada.

iii India
The service records of European officers and soldiers of the Honourable East India Company's service, and of the Indian (Imperial) Army are mainly preserved at the India Office Library, but the service records of the regular army in India will be found with the other army records in the PRO. You will often find the name of the wife as next of kin in the casualty returns when a soldier has died (WO 25). There are musters of regiments in India from 1883 to 1889 (WO 16), but there are none for the Artillery or the Engineers. When a soldier was discharged on his return home, you should find a record of this in the depot musters of his regiment (WO 67), in the Musters of the Victoria Hospital, Netley (for the years 1863–1878) (WO 12) or in the Musters of the Discharge Depot, Gosport (1875–1889) (WO 16).

iv Soldiers' Wills
When soldiers died abroad, their wills were usually proved in the Prerogative Court of Canterbury, and there are many thousand such wills in the PRO (see III/3 above).

v Regimental Records
Most regiments have their own museums, some of which have archival collections; a search may be productive. The National Army Museum and the Army Museums Ogilby Trust also have collections.

vi Deserters
There are War Office registers of deserters (1799–1852) (WO 25) which contain personal details and the punishment awarded to deserters who were caught, and

certificates among the papers of the Tax Receivers for the award of the bounty for catching deserters (from the 1720s) (E 182).

vii Chaplains
Because of the dearth of War Office records of chaplains, look first at *Crockford's Clerical Directory*, then the diocesan register of ordinands in the appropriate diocesan record office, and the Oxford and Cambridge *Alumni*. You may find something in the *Gentleman's Magazine*. In the PRO there are entries of payments to Chaplains, 1805–1843 (WO 25) and letters from chaplains, 1808–1836, in the Chaplain General's Letter Books (WO 40).

d Other Military Formations

i The Militia
From medieval times, able-bodied men aged between 16 and 60 were liable to perform military service within their counties, and occasionally outside them, in times of need. From the 1540s, the records of musters were returned to the Secretaries of State, and many of these, with some earlier ones from 1522 onwards, are scattered among various classes in the PRO (E 36, E 101, E 315, SP 1, SP 2, SP 10, SP 12, SP 14, SP 16, SP 17). Some muster books, however, were retained by the deputy lieutenants of the counties, and these are now in private collections or county record offices.

A few militia soldiers qualified for pensions during the French Revolutionary and Napoleonic Wars, and their discharge certificates among the ordinary soldiers' documents (WO 97) give their place of birth and age on enlistment. There are also lists of militia men, and wives and children who were eligible for pensions among the subsidiary documents to the Receiver's Accounts (E 182), but there are no indexes, so it is a question of wading through sacks of documents. You would do better to look in the War Office and Home Office records for the militia in the late eighteenth century and the nineteenth century (HO 51, WO 13, WO 68).

ii The Territorial Army
The Territorial Force was established in 1908 by amalgamating the Militia, Yeomanry (mounted volunteers) and Volunteer Force (infantry), to provide defences for Britain when the regular army had gone abroad. It became the Territorial Army in 1921. Most of the records are held locally; the muster rolls of some London and Middlesex Volunteer and Territorial regiments (1860–1912) are in the PRO (WO 70).

iii Military Police
The Military Police became a separate organisaton from the middle of the nineteenth century, and enquiries should be sent direct to them.

See also IV/16 below for deaths abroad, and IV/24 below for prisoners of war.

Bibliography

Books

Crockford's Clerical Directory (Oxford, from 1858)
C Firth and G Davis, *The Regimental History of Cromwell's Army*, (Oxford, 1940)
J Foster, *Alumini Oxonienses, 1500–1886* (Oxford, 1891)
The Gentleman's Magazine (London, 1731–1903)
G Hamilton Edwards, *In Search of Army Ancestry* (London, 1977)
M S Giuseppi, *Guide to the Manuscripts preserved in the Public Record Office* (London, 1923–1924)
M E S Laws, *Battery Records of the Royal Artillery*, vol. I, *1716–1859, vol. II, 1859–1877* (Woolwich, 1952, 1970)
E E Rich, 'The Population of Elizabethan England', *Economic History Review*, 2nd series, vol. II (1949–1950), pp. 247–265
J and J A Venn, *Alumni Cantabrigienses, from the Earliest Times to 1900* (Cambridge, 1922–1927)
T Wise, *A Guide to Military Museums* (Hemel Hempstead, 1971)

Published Finding Aids

Alphabetical Guide to War Office and other Military Records preserved in the Public Record Office, PRO Lists and Indexes, vol. LIII (1931)
The Army List (London, annually from 1754)
Calendar of State Papers, Domestic Series (London, 1856–1972)
T W J Connolly, *List of Officers, Royal Engineers, 1660–1898* (London, 1898)
C Dalton, *English Army Lists and Commission Registers, 1661–1714* (London, 1892–1904)
C Dalton, *Waterloo Roll* (London, 2nd edn., 1904)
E Dwelly, *Waterloo Muster Rolls: Cavalry* (Fleet, Hants, 1934)
H G Hart, *Army Lists* (from 1840)
J Kane, *List of Officers, Royal Artillery, 1716–1899* (London, 4th edn., 1900)
K O N Kingsley-Foster, *Military General Service Medal, 1793–1814* (London, 1947)
Letters and Papers of Henry VIII (London, 1920–1929) e.g. for Militia musters
Lists of War Office Records, PRO Lists and Indexes, vol. XXVIII (1908), PRO Supplementary Lists and Indexes, vol. VIII (1968)
Officers died in the Great War (London, 1921), the Imperial War Museum, London
E Peacock, *The Army List of Roundheads and Cavaliers* (London, 2nd edn., 1874)
Soldiers died in the Great War, 80 parts (London, 1921–1922), the Imperial War Museum, London

Unpublished Finding Aids

Index to deserters' certificates for Bedfordshire, Buckinghamshire, Berkshire, Cambridgeshire, Cheshire and Middlesex, card index
Index of Names of Officers who appear in the Army Lists 1702–1752 (WO 64 and WO 65) card index

Exchequer and Audit Department
AO 1   Declared Accounts, 1536–1828
AO 2   Declared and Passed Accounts, 1803–1848
AO 3   Accounts, Various, 1539–1886

Exchequer: Treasury of Receipt
E 36   Books, 13th to 18th century (Militia musters, E 36/16–55a)

Exchequer: King's Remembrancer
E 101   Various Accounts, Henry II to George III (Militia musters, E 101/58 *et seq.*, 549)
E 157   Licences to pass beyond the Seas, Elizabeth I to 1677
E 182   Receivers' Accounts of Land and Assessed Taxes: Subsidiary Documents, 1689–1830

Exchequer: Augmentation Office
E 315   Miscellaneous Books, 12th to 18th century (Militia musters, E 315/464, 466)

Exchequer of Receipt
E 403   Enrolments and Registers of Issues, Henry III to 1834

Home Office
HO 51   Military Entry Books, 1782–1840

Paymaster General's Office
PMG 3   Army Establishment, Retired Full Pay and General Officers' Pay and Allowances, 1813–1920
PMG 4   Army Establishment Half Pay, 1737–1921
PMG 5   Commissariat Half Pay, Pensions, etc., 1854–1855
PMG 6   Army Establishment, Foreign Half Pay, Pensions, etc., 1822–1885
PMG 7   Army Establishment, Hanover, Foreign Half Pay, Pensions, etc., 1843–1862
PMG 8   Army Establishment, Hanover, Chelsea Out-Pensions, 1844–1877
PMG 9   Army Establishment, Pensions for Wounds, 1814–1921
PMG 10   Army Establishment, Compassionate List and Royal Bounty, 1812–1916
PMG 11   Army Establishment, Widows' Pensions, 1810–1920
PMG 12   Ordnance Half Pay, Pensions, etc., 1836–1875
PMG 13   Militia, Yeomanry and Volunteers Allowances, 1793–1927
PMG 14   Army Establishment, Miscellaneous Books, 1720–1861
PMG 33   Army Establishment Warrant Officers Non-Effective Pensions, 1909–1928
PMG 34   Army Establishment Schoolmistresses and Nurses Pensions, 1909–1928
PMG 35   Army Establishment Rewards for Distinguished Services, etc., 1873–1941
PMG 36   Army Establishment Rewards to Warrant Officers for Distinguished or Meritorious Services, 1909–1928
PMG 42   Ministry of Pensions Disability Retired Pay, Gratuities, etc., 1917–1920

PMG 43   Ministry of Pensions Supplementary Allowances and Special Grants, 1916–1920

PMG 44   Ministry of Pensions, Pensions to Relatives to Deceased Officers, 1916–1920

PMG 45   Ministry of Pensions Widows' Pensions, 1917–1919

PMG 46   Ministry of Pensions Childrens' Allowances, 1916–1920

PMG 47   Ministry of Pensions, Relatives of Missing Officers, 1915–1920

PMG 57   Army Establishment Civil Officers, Artificers, etc., Superannuation, 1857–1920

State Paper Office

SP 1   State Papers, Henry VIII, General, Domestic and Foreign, 1509–1547

SP 2   State Papers, Henry VIII, Folios, Domestic and Foreign, 1516–1539

SP 10   State Papers, Domestic, Edward VI, 1547–1553

SP 12   State Papers, Domestic, Elizabeth I, 1558–1603

SP 14   State Papers, Domestic, James I, 1603–1625

SP 16   State Papers, Domestic, Charles I, 1625–1649

SP 17   State Papers, Domestic, Charles I, Cases, 1625–1649

SP 28   State Papers, Domestic, Commonwealth Exchequer, 1642–1660

War Office

WO 10   Muster Books and Pay Lists, Artillery, 1708–1878

WO 11   Muster Books and Pay Lists, Engineers, 1816–1878

WO 12   Muster Books and Pay Lists, General, 1732–1878

WO 13   Muster Books and Pay Lists, Militia and Volunteers, 1780–1878

WO 16   Muster Books and Pay Lists, New Series, 1878–1898

WO 17   Monthly Returns, 1759–1865

WO 25   Registers, Various, 1660–1938 (out pension records)

WO 31   Memoranda Papers, Commander in Chief, 1793–1870

WO 40   Selected Unnumbered Papers, 1753–1859

WO 42   Returns: Certificates of Birth, etc., 1755–1908

WO 54   Ordnance Office Registers, 1594–1871

WO 64   Manuscript Army Lists, 1702–1823

WO 67   Depot Description Books, 1768–1908

WO 68   Militia Records, 1759–1925

WO 69   Artillery Records of Service, 1756–1906

WO 70   Volunteer and Territorial Records, 1860–1912

WO 73   Monthly Returns: Distribution of the Army, 1859–1946

WO 76   Returns: Records of Officers' Services, 1755–1954

WO 96   Militia Attestation Papers, 1806–1915

WO 97   Soldiers' Documents, 1760–1900 (in part to 1913)

WO 100   Campaign Medals, 1791–1912

WO 108   South African War: Papers, 1899–1905

WO 116   Royal Hospital, Chelsea, Admission Books, Disability and Royal Artillery, 1715–1913

WO 117   Royal Hospital, Chelsea, Admission Books, Length of Service, 1823–1920

WO 118   Royal Hospital, Kilmainham, Admission Books, 1704–1922

WO 119   Royal Hospital, Kilmainham, Discharge Documents of Pensioners, 1783–1822

WO 121   Royal Hospital, Chelsea, Discharge Documents of Pensioners, 1787–1813

WO 122   Royal Hospital, Chelsea, Foreigners' Regiments, 1816–1817

WO 126   South African War, Local Armed Forces, Enrolment Forms, 1899–1902

WO 127   South African War, Local Armed Forces, Nominal Rolls, 1899–1902

WO 128   South African War, Imperial Yeomanry, Soldiers' Documents, 1899–1902

WO 131   Royal Hospital Chelsea, Documents of Soldiers awarded deferred Pensions, 1838–1896

WO 143   Duke of York's School and Royal Hibernian School, 1801–1958

WO 156   Registers of Baptisms and Banns of Marriage, 1865–1958

WO 165–WO 179   War of 1939–1945 War Diaries, various theatres

2 Sailors in the Royal Navy

For men serving before the Restoration (1660), no systematic service records survive in the PRO. Anything there is will be found among the State Papers (SP), which are best approached through the series of published *Calendars*, cited above (p. 31). For the service records of ratings who enlisted after 1891 and officers after the 1880s, you should write to Naval Personnel Records. For the period 1660–c. 1890, the relevant records are in the PRO. Naval personnel fell into three categories, commissioned officers (almost invariably from the gentry and upper classes), warrant officers (professional seamen, usually of humble birth), and ratings. Commissioned officers first went to sea as midshipmen (warrant officers).

a Commissioned Officers
These men held their rank by commission from the Crown, and their principal task was to bring the ship to battle. They were, in order of rank (but with variations at different times), Admiral of the Fleet, Admiral, Vice-Admiral, Rear Admiral, Commodore, Captain, Commander, Lieutenant-Commander, Lieutenant, Sub-Lieutenant. But, beware, officers are not always exactly described in non-naval records, and terminology can in any case be confusing:

A man referred to as 'Captain X' may be:
1 A post-Captain in rank (1700 onwards).
2 Holding a Captain's commission (before 1700).
3 A Commander, holding a command (before 20th century).
4 A Commander, not holding a command (1827–c. 1900).
5 A Lieutenant, holding a command (before 20th century).
6 A Captain, Royal Marines, Royal Marine Artillery or Royal Marine Light Infantry.
7 Master of a merchantman (East India Co. or 20th century).

A man referred to as 'the Captain of the Y'* may be:
1 A post-Captain.
2 A commander, holding a command.
3 A Lieutenant-Commander (1914 onwards) holding a command.
4 A Lieutenant holding a command.
5 Any other rank holding a command.

A man referred to as 'Commander X' may be:
1 A Commander in rank (1794 onwards).
2 A post-Captain (rarely, 17–18th centuries).
3 A Lieutenant in Command (18th century, rarely 19th century).
4 A Lieutenant-Commander (1914 onwards).

A man referred to as 'Commander of the Y' may be:
1 The Captain, of whatever rank (before 20th century).
2 The Commander, i.e. executive officer (1827 onwards).

A man referred to as 'Lieutenant-Commander X' may be:
1 A Lieutenant in command (18–19th centuries).
2 A Lieutenant-Commander (1914 onwards).

A man referred to as 'Lieutenant X' may be:
1 A Lieutenant in rank.
2 Holding a Lieutenant's commission (before 1700).
3 A Lieutenant, Royal Marines, Royal Marine Artillery or Royal Marine
Light Infantry.
4 A Sub-Lieutenant R.N.

A man addressed as 'Commodore X' may be:
1 A Commodore R.N., otherwise addressed as 'Captain'.
2 Senior Master of a convoy or merchant fleet, otherwise addressed as
'Captain' (East India Company and 20th Century) or 'Mr.'.

A man addressed as 'Admiral X ' may be:
1 An Admiral (of the Red, White or Blue before 1963).
2 A Vice-Admiral (likewise).
3 A Rear-Admiral (likewise).
4 A 'Yellow Admiral' of any of the above ranks; i.e. an officer promoted on
half pay or after retirement to a rank never exercised except for purposes of
pay and pension.

An outline of an officer's career can usually be constructed from the various
printed and typsecript compilations available, such as the *Navy List* and naval
biographies. You should then try looking at the Lieutenants' Passing Certificates
(1691–1902) (ADM 6, ADM 13, ADM 107), which give information on the

---

* i.e. a ship; such titles as 'Captain of the Foretop', 'Captain of the Hold', indicate jobs held by
senior petty-officers.

candidate's previous career; and the Records and Returns of Officer's Services (ADM 9, ADM 10, ADM 196). Once you know the name of the ship on which a man served, the Captains' Logs (ADM 51) may be useful; Lieutenants' Logs are held by the National Maritime Museum. You may also find references to an officer in the Indexes (ADM 12) to the Admiralty Correspondence (ADM 1), although, obviously, the higher a man was in rank the more likely is this to be the case.

b Warrant Officers

Warrant officers had authority in their own departments by virtue of a warrant from the captain, earned by their particular skills. They included such men as the master (responsible for navigating the ship, under the captain's orders) and his mates, boatswain (in charge of the rigging), gunner, engineer, carpenter, sailmaker, surgeon, cooper, chaplain, and midshipmen, who were usually boys, in charge of a group of men and hoping to become lieutenants.

The best place to start looking for records of warrant officers is among their records of service (ADM 29, ADM 104), which give brief details of all men superannuated after 1802, and who therefore started their careers well back into the eighteenth century. There are some warrant officers mentioned in the records of officer's services (ADM 196), in the Seniority Lists (ADM 118) and the Warrant Books (ADM 6, ADM 11). Censuses were sometimes taken of some types of warrant officer (ADM 6, ADM 11), and almost all of them had to take some kind of examination which resulted in registers of their certificates of competency (ADM 6, ADM 13, ADM 106). Masters and surgeons also kept logs (ADM 52, ADM 101); the latter sometimes contain vivid accounts of places visited. There are references to chaplains in Chatham Chest records (ADM 82), Full Pay Ledgers (ADM 24), and Accountant General Registers (ADM 30). Some more recent records of chaplains are still held by the Chaplain of the Fleet.

c Ratings

For the service records of an ordinary seaman before 1853, you will be in difficulty unless you know the name of the ship on which the man served at a particular time. If you do not, but think that your ancestor was involved in a specific battle, then you could try the Medal Rolls (ADM 171) which are arranged by campaign. If you know where a man was serving at a given time, but not in which ship, you can find out which ships were there at the date in question by looking at the List Books (ADM 8).

If the name of the ship is known the Ships' Musters (from 1667) (ADM 36–ADM 39) can be used, and by working through preceding and succeeding musters a more or less complete record of service established. You may find the man's age and place of birth in the muster, and if a Description Book survives with the Muster you will find many more personal details. If there is no muster, the Ships' Pay Books (ADM 31–ADM 35) will at least confirm a man's presence on board. You will find the full record of service of a seaman superannuated after 1802 in the Warrant Officers' and Seamen's Services (ADM 29).

In 1853, Continuous Service Engagement was introduced, and seamen were assigned Continuous Service (CS) numbers. When a man entered the service, a certificate was completed giving his date and place of birth, description and ship, and brief records of his subsequent service were later added. This system ended in 1872 and was replaced by new Official Numbers, which referred to the records of Seamen's Services. These two series up to 1891 are at the PRO (ADM 139, ADM 188), but thereafter it only holds records of ratings serving with armoured cars in Russia from 1915 to 1917 (ADM 116/1717).

d Sea Fencibles
Sea Fencibles were the naval equivalent of the Militia: forces raised for local defensive service only. There are pay lists for the period 1798–1810 (ADM 28).

e Coastguards
Coastguard service records, 1816–1923 (ADM 175), and Muster Books, 1824–1857 (ADM 119), are among the Admiralty records, and there are pension papers in the Paymaster General's records (PMG 23, PMG 70).

f Other sources: Pensions, Wills, etc.
Ledgers recording Full and Half Pay of officers (ADM 22, ADM 24, PMG 15), pensions of officers and men, and widows' pensions may be used to supplement the sources above, though they rarely record genealogical information except in any explanatory note of a first or last payment. If you can find no other means of establishing a date of death, you may at least learn an approximate date.

To identify any relevant pension records it is necessary to know the reason for which the pension was awarded: wounds, disability, meritorious conduct, poverty, widow's pension, etc. Payments are recorded in many places. There are some for the years 1654–1660 in the Admiralty Accounting Departments' Bill Books (ADM 18), and others for wounded men in the Chatham Chest Records (ADM 82). The majority of pensions were paid by Greenwich Hospital, which were recorded in the various registers of that institution (ADM 73, ADM 165, ADM 166, PMG 15, PMG 16, PMG 18–PMG 20, PMG 23–PMG 25, PMG 56, PMG 69–PMG 72). From 1822 to 1912 (by the Statute 46 and 47 Vict., c. 32) Greenwich Hospital pensions included payments to the widows and children of warrant officers, petty officers, and ratings who died in service but not in action (ADM 166). In 1916 responsibility for payments under the Act passed to the Ministry of Pensions, whose records are with those of the Paymaster General (PMG 42–PMG 47).

Where papers survive in support of applications for a pension or bounty they can be valuable genealogical sources. The applications for widows' pensions (ADM 6, ADM 22) for instance, include marriage certificates, and give the date of the husband's death. You may also find material of use in the In-Letters (ADM 65), Admission Papers (ADM 73) and papers on widows' charities (ADM 6, ADM 68) of Greenwich Hospital. The Navy Board Bounty Papers (ADM 106) are petitions from poor widows, orphans and mothers of officers and men killed or mortally wounded at sea. They often give precise details of the death, and are supported by parochial certificates of marriage, baptism or kinship as appropriate.

There is a large number of seamen's wills among the Admiralty records (ADM 48), as well as among the records of the Prerogative Court of Canterbury (see III/3 above). After 1815, if a seaman died with wages totalling less than £20 owing to him, his will was not eligible for proving in the PCC, so you should look for it in the records of the appropriate local court. Besides the original wills, there are copies of wills and original letters of administration (1800–1860) among the Seamen's, Officers' and Civilians' Effects Papers (ADM 44, ADM 45). These records are more complete than the series of wills, and are particularly useful for the genealogist as you will often find birth and marriage certificates attached to the grant.

For prisoners of war see IV/24 below.

Bibliography

Books

J Campbell and W Stevenson, *Lives of the British Admirals* (London, 1917)
J Charnock, *Biographia Navalis* (London, 1794–1798)
Dictionary of National Biography
J Marshall, *Royal Naval Biography* (London, 1823–1830)
W R O'Byrne, *A Naval Biographical Dictionary* (London, 1849)

Published Finding Aids

Calendar of State Papers, Domestic Series (London, 1856–1972)
Commissioned Sea Officers of the Royal Navy, 1660–1815 (London, 1954)
A G Kealy, *Chaplains of the Royal Navy, 1626–1903* (Portsmouth, 1905)
List of Sea Officers (London, 1800–1824)
The Navy List (London, annually from 1814)
D Steel, *Navy List* (London, 1782–1817)

Unpublished Finding Aids

Card index of seamen's wills (ADM 48), A–H only
E H B Fairbrother, Index of Chaplains, MS
Index of lieutenants' passing certificates, 1789–1818 (ADM 107), TS
A G Kealy, List of Chaplains, Royal Navy, 1626–1816

Records

Admiralty
ADM 1   Admiralty and Secretariat Papers, 1660–1969 (index in ADM 12)
ADM 6   Various Registers, Returns and Certificates, 1673–1859
ADM 8   List Books, 1673–1893
ADM 9   Original Returns of Officers' Services, 1817–1848 (index in ADM 10)
ADM 10   Indexes and Compilations, Series I (includes index to ADM 9), 1660–1851

ADM 11	Indexes and Compilations, Series II (includes commissioned and warrant officers' records), 1741–1869
ADM 12	Indexes and Compilations, Series III (includes digests and indexes to ADM 1 and ADM 116), 1660–1938
ADM 13	Supplementary Papers, 1803–1902
ADM 18	Accounting Departments' Bill Books, 1642–1831
ADM 22	Registers of Salaries and Pensions, 1734–1858
ADM 24	Officers' Full Pay Registers, 1795–1872
ADM 28	Sea Fencibles Pay Lists, 1798–1810
ADM 29	Warrant Officers' and Seamens' Services, 1802–1871
ADM 30	Accounting Departments' Registers, 1689–1836
ADM 31	Ships' Pay Books: Controller's 1691–1710
ADM 32	Ships' Pay Books: Ticket Office, 1692–1856
ADM 33	Ships' Pay Books: Treasurer's, Series I, 1669–1778
ADM 34	Ships' Pay Books: Treasurer's, Series II, 1766–1785
ADM 35	Ships' Pay Books: Treasurer's, Series III, 1777–1832
ADM 36	Ships' Musters, Series I, 1688–1808
ADM 37	Ships' Musters, Series II, 1804–1842
ADM 38	Ships' Musters, Series III, 1793–1878
ADM 39	Ships' Musters, Series IV, 1667–1798
ADM 44	Seamen's Effects Papers, 1800–1860 (index in ADM 141)
ADM 45	Officers' and Civilians' Effects Papers, 1830–1860 (index in ADM 141)
ADM 48	Seamen's Wills, 1786–1882 (index in ADM 142)
ADM 50	Admirals' Journals, 1702–1916
ADM 51	Captains' Logs, 1669–1852
ADM 52	Masters' Logs, 1672–1840
ADM 65	Greenwich Hospital In-Letters, 1702–1869
ADM 68	Greenwich Hospital Accounts, 1696–1865
ADM 73	Greenwich Hospital Registers, 1704–1966
ADM 82	Chatham Chest, 1617–1807
ADM 101	Medical Journals, 1785–1880
ADM 104	Medical Departments' Registers, 1774–1866
ADM 106	Navy Board Records, 1659–1837
ADM 107	Navy Board Passing Certificates, 1691–1848
ADM 116	Admiralty and Secretariat Cases, 1852–1949 (index in ADM 12)
ADM 118	Seniority Lists, 1717–1850
ADM 119	Ships' Musters: Coastguard and Revenue Cruisers, 1824–1857
ADM 139	Accounting Departments: Continuous Service Engagement Books, 1853–1872
ADM 141	Registers of Seamen's Effects Papers (index to ADM 44 and ADM 45), 1802–1861
ADM 142	Registers of Seamen's Wills (index to ADM 48), 1786–1909
ADM 165	Greenwich Hospital Registers of Pensions to Naval and Marine Officers and Greenwich Hospital Staff, 1871–1961
ADM 166	Greenwich Hospital Registers of Pensions to Widows of Seamen and Marines, 1882–1949
ADM 171	Medal Rolls, 1793–1914

ADM 175   Coastguard Records of Service, 1816–1923
ADM 188   Registers of Seamen's Services, 1873–1895*
ADM 196   Records of Officers' Services, 1777–1954
ADM 240   Royal Naval Reserve: Records of Officers' Services, 1862–1960

Paymaster General's Office

PMG 15   Naval Establishment, Half Pay, Retired Pay and Unattached Pay, 1836–1920
PMG 16   Naval Establishment, Pensions for Miscellaneous Services, Wounds, Widows, etc., 1836–1920
PMG 18   Naval Establishment, Compassionate List, 1837–1921
PMG 19   Pensions for Widows of Naval Officers, 1836–1929
PMG 20   Pensions for Widows of Marine Officers and Relatives of Naval and Marine Officers, killed on duty, 1870–1919
PMG 23   Coastguard: Civil Pensions, 1855–1935
PMG 24   Salaried Officers' Civil Pensions, 1836–1918
PMG 25   Artificers' and Labourers' Civil Pensions, 1836–1928
PMG 42   War of 1914–1918, Ministry of Pensions, Disability Retired Pay, Gratuities, etc., 1917–1920
PMG 43   War of 1914–1918, Ministry of Pensions, Supplementary Allowances and Special Grants, 1916–1920
PMG 44   War of 1914–1918, Ministry of Pensions, Pensions to Relatives of Deceased Officers, 1916–1920
PMG 45   War of 1914–1918, Ministry of Pensions, Widows' Pensions, 1916–1919
PMG 46   War of 1914–1918, Ministry of Pensions, Children's Allowances, 1916–1920
PMG 47   War of 1914–1918, Ministry of Pensions, Relatives of Missing Officers, 1915–1920
PMG 56   Naval Establishment, Warlike Operations, Pensions, etc., 1914–1928
PMG 69   Engineers, Subordinate and Warrant Officers, etc., Pensions, 1874–1924
PMG 70   Greenwich Hospital Pensions and Civil Superannuation Allowances, 1866–1928
PMG 71   Naval Pensions, 1846–1921
PMG 72   Widows and Dependents of Seamen and Marines, Pensions, 1921–1926

SP   State Paper Office

3 Royal Marines

Soldiers were recruited exclusively for sea service from 1690. Until 1755, control of marine regiments was committed to military or naval authorities, depending on whether the men were on shore or at sea. The records of the Marines are thus divided among the papers of the Admiralty (ADM), State Paper Office (SP) and War Office (WO) during this period.

---

* This includes full service records for anyone who enlisted pre or during 1891.

**III Sketch of a forest official from a roll of forest
proceedings relating to the Forest of Dean.
Late thirteenth century** (E 32/31)

**IV Drawing of a King's Messenger, with a footman,
from an account of messengers' expenses.
Fourteenth century** (E 101/309/11)

On 3 April 1755 an Order in Council approved the raising of 5000 Marines, who were grouped in 50 'companies', each of which was assigned to one of three 'Grand Divisions', quartered respectively at Chatham, Plymouth and Portsmouth, under the control of the Board of Admiralty. The number of companies steadily grew and the Marines were never again disbanded. They were designated 'Royal' Marines by George III in an order dated 29 April 1802. From 1805 to 1869 there was a further Division, quartered at Woolwich. In 1848 the Portsmouth Division moved to Forton barracks, Gosport, and in 1861 a Depot was established at Walmer, Kent (later the Royal Marine Depot, Deal). The 'companies' within each division were purely administrative units, which bore no relation to the tactical units formed when the Marines were on active service. These tactical units might contain men of many separate divisions.

In 1804 separate companies of artillery were authorised (again by Order in Council), each to be attached to one of the existing divisions. (Before this date men from the Royal Artillery had been called on to serve at sea when required.) The total number of artillery companies rose and fell according to demand: for a time in the 1830s, for example, there were only two such companies, both attached to the Portsmouth Division. The whole corps was named the Royal Marine Light Infantry from 1855, but in 1859 the Royal Marine Artillery was formed into a separate Division for which Eastney barracks was built. In 1923 the RMLI ('Red Marines') and RMA ('Blue Marines') were merged into a single corps of Royal Marines.

a Officers

No records of officers' services for men appointed before 1793 have survived, although confirmation of a commission or appointment may sometimes be found. For officers commissioned after 1793 you should look first in the Records of Officers' Services (ADM 196), which give full details of service, and sometimes also include the name and profession of the officer's father. These records, however, are still incomplete until about 1837, as officers who served only for a short period into the nineteenth century are not recorded. These volumes are open to public inspection 30 years after the last discharge date of an officer in a volume. The volumes for officers appointed after 1906 have final dates which fall within this closure period, so records are only available of officers appointed before 1906. Enquiries about officers appointed later should be sent to the Commandant General of the Royal Marines.

Where no full record of service survives, you may learn something from the Lists of Marine Officers, two incomplete sets of which are among the Seniority Lists (ADM 118) and the Lists of Officers (ADM 192). The *Navy Lists* also include Marine officers. Some further information may occasionally be gleaned from the Commission and Subsistence Books (ADM 96) among the Marine Pay Office Registers, but the Commissions and Appointments (ADM 6) contain no helpful details for genealogists. In 1822 a survey was made of half pay officers, which gives their age and little else (ADM 6/409).

Separate records of warrant officers have survived only in one volume among the other records of Officers' Services (ADM 196/67). If the officer you are looking for is not there, your best chance is that he became a commissioned officer later.

b Other Ranks

Records of service for other ranks survive in abundance, but you may find it difficult to trace an individual unless you know his division or company. There was no central system of numbering Marines until 1884, so until then men of the same name can be differentiated only by their company number. The records are mainly arranged by divisions, but if you know your ancestor's company you can ascertain his division from tables in the Lists of Officers. If you cannot determine his division, you will have to search through the records of each in turn. Men normally remained with the company in which they enlisted unless promoted, when they were sometimes transferred.

There is a series of various registers, known collectively as Description Books (ADM 158), which may be helpful. They are arranged by date of attestation (i.e. enlistment) and by the initial letter of the man's surname, and give age, parish of birth and a physical description, but not the ships or battalions in which a man served. They cover several years in each volume, and an individual may be in more than one book, so they can be useful if you know only a man's name.

If you know the date of a man's discharge, you may do better to start with the Attestation Forms (ADM 157) which were completed when a man enlisted, but until 1883 were filed by the discharge date, and arranged by divisions and initial letters. You should find on these forms some notes on service, and perhaps the date and circumstances of death.

In 1884 each man was given his own distinctive number, and Records of Service were introduced (ADM 159). You will have a long search if you do not know a man's number as there is no key and they are only roughly chronological by date of enlistment. The informatioin provided once you have found your man is extensive: date and place of birth, trade, religion, date and place of enlistment, physical description, a full record of service, and comments on conduct, promotions etc. The records in the PRO cover men enlisted up to 1901; for men enlisted after that date you should write to the Royal Marines' Drafting and Record Office.

You may find that a look in the Effective and Subsistence Lists (ADM 96) is helpful in providing hints for other places to search. They contain no personal details but list men for pay and expenses and may indicate, for example, that a man served abroad. If you know that a man served on a particular ship and when, you should consult the Ship's Musters (ADM 36–ADM 39), and if you think he may have been decorated you could look in the Medal Rolls (ADM 171). For the Second World War there are War Diaries (ADM 202), arranged by unit, ship or operation; for commando units a look in the Combined Operations Headquarters records may be worthwhile (DEFE 2).

c Other Records

i Divisions
There are some records of the various divisions in the PRO, which include such useful genealogical material as registers of births, marriages and deaths and discharge and embarkation books, as well as correspondence (ADM 81, ADM 183–ADM 185, ADM 193).

ii Courts Martial
Registers of Courts Martial survive for the Portsmouth Division from 1834 and for the Plymouth Division from 1836, together with those for certain units serving overseas (ADM 194). Some earlier papers will be found with those of Royal Naval trials (ADM 13). These records are closed for a period of 75 years after the date of the last entry in the volume.

iii Pensions
These are to be found among the Royal Naval pensions, with the records of Greenwich Hospital and the Paymaster General (see IV/2 above).

iv Central Records
There are separate sections among the Admiralty In- (ADM 1) and Out-letters (ADM 2) for correspondence and papers on policy matters, including recruitment and deployment, concerning the Marines. You will also find correspondence of the Marine Pay Office (ADM 96) until 1862, although it became part of the office of the Accountant General of the Navy in 1831 (which in turn became part of the Paymaster General's Office in 1835).

The Royal Marine Office, now the Commandant General's Office, kept letter books, first general (ADM 56), then from 1868 classified by correspondent: divisions (ADM 57–ADM 63), Admiralty (ADM 191), War Office (ADM 200). There are also some records of the Office among the General Standing Orders (ADM 64).

Bibliography

Books

H E Blumberg, *Britain's Sea Soldiers, 1914–1919* (Devonport, 1927)
C Field, *Britain's Sea Soldiers* (Liverpool, 1924)
E Fraser and L G Carr-Laughton, *Royal Marine Artillery* (London, 1930)
A C Hampshire, *The Royal Marines' Tercentenary* (London, 1964)
R B Lockhart, *The Marines were there* (London, 1950)
J L Moulton, *The Royal Marines* (London, 1973)
P C Smith, *Per Mare Per Terram* (St Ives, Hunts, 1974)

Published Finding Aids

Alphabetical Guide to the War Office and other materials, PRO Lists and Indexes, vol. LIII (1931)
Navy List (London, annually from 1814)

See list under Royal Navy, above IV/2

Admiralty

ADM 2	Admiralty and Secretariat, Out Letters, 1659–1859
ADM 56	Royal Marine Office, Letter Books: General, 1806–1868
ADM 57	Royal Marine Office, Letter Books: Woolwich, 1868–1869
ADM 58	Royal Marine Office, Letter Books: Chatham, 1868–1884
ADM 59	Royal Marine Office, Letter Books: Royal Marine Artillery, 1868–1884
ADM 60	Royal Marine Office, Letter Books: Gosport, 1868–1884
ADM 61	Royal Marine Office, Letter Books: Plymouth, 1868–1884
ADM 62	Royal Marine Office, Letter Books: Deal, 1868–1884
ADM 63	Royal Marine Office, Letter Books: Miscellaneous, 1834–1889
ADM 64	Royal Marines, General Standing Orders, 1888–1936
ADM 81	Royal Marines, Woolwich Division, 1805–1869
ADM 96	Marine Pay Office, 1688–1862
ADM 157	Royal Marines, Attestation Forms, 1790–1883
ADM 158	Royal Marines, Description Books, c. 1750–1888
ADM 159	Royal Marines, Registers of Service, 1842–1905
ADM 183	Royal Marines, Chatham Division, 1755–1941
ADM 184	Royal Marines, Plymouth Division, 1760–1941
ADM 185	Royal Marines, Portsmouth Division, 1763–1941
ADM 191	Royal Marine Office, Letter Books: Admiralty, 1826–1884
ADM 192	Royal Marines, Lists of Officers, 1760–1886
ADM 193	Royal Marines, Miscellaneous, 1761–1918
ADM 194	Courts Martial Registers, 1812–1916
ADM 200	Royal Marine Office, Letter Books: War Office, 1868–1884
ADM 201	Royal Marine Office, Correspondence and Papers, 1761–1928
ADM 202	Royal Marines, War Diaries, 1939–1946

Ministry of Defence

DEFE 2	Combined Operations Headquarters Records, 1937–1951

War Office

WO 1	In Letters, 1732–1868
WO 3	Out Letters, Commander in Chief, 1765–1868
WO 4	Out Letters, Secretary at War, 1684–1861
WO 6	Out Letters, Secretary of State, 1793–1859
WO 26	Miscellany Books, 1670–1817
WO 32	Registered Papers, General, 1855–1971
WO 33	Reports and Miscellaneous Papers, 1853–1943
WO 44	Ordnance Office, In Letters, 1682–1873
WO 47	Ordnance Office, Minutes, 1644–1856
WO 81	Judge Advocate General's Office, Letter Books, 1715–1900

4 Royal Air Force and Royal Flying Corps

The PRO holds no RAF personnel records. The Air Ministry group of records consist of central office papers and operational records, which often include the names of men and women serving but it would be a long job to find any particular person. Personnel records of all RAF ranks will be released to relatives only on application to RAF Personnel Management. Other records such as notification of casualties, and honours are held by RAF Officers' Records.

You will find some officers' pensions among the Paymaster General's records for the period 1916–1920 (PMG 42, PMG 44), and information on prisoners of war among Air Ministry and Foreign Office files (AIR 40, AIR 46, AIR 49, FO 916). It may also be worth looking at the RAF monographs and narratives (AIR 41), and the citations and grants of commissions and honours (AIR 2, AIR 30).

Records

Air Ministry
AIR 2   Correspondence, 1887–1969
AIR 30   Submission Papers, 1918–1946
AIR 40   Directorate of Intelligence and other Intelligence Papers, 1923–1947
AIR 41   Air Historical Branch, Monographs and Narratives, 1942–1950
AIR 46   Air Missions, 1939–1960
AIR 49   History of RAF Medical Services, Narratives and Drafts, 1919–1951
Foreign Office
FO 916   War of 1939–1945, Consular (War) Department: Prisoners of War and Internees, 1940–1946
Paymaster General's Office
PMG 42   War of 1914–1918, Ministry of Pensions, Disability Retired Pay, Gratuities, etc., 1916–1920
PMG 44   War of 1914–1918, Ministry of Pensions, Pensions to Relatives of Deceased Officers, 1916–1920

5 Royal Irish Constabulary

This peace keeping force was, in effect, created in 1836 when the local groups of sub constables were united under the command of an Inspector-General. This force was given the title Royal Irish Constabulary in 1867. It was responsible for the whole of Ireland with the exception of Dublin, and so was disbanded in August 1922.

The main series of service records for members of the Royal Irish Constabulary is among the Home Office papers (HO 184). The registers are arranged by service number, but there are separate alphabetical indexes. They normally give name, age, height, religious affiliation, native country, trade, marital status, native country of wife (but not her name), date of appointment, countries in which the man served, length of service and date of retirement or death, but no information about parentage.

Pensions and allowances granted to officers, men and staff, and to their widows and children are recorded among the Paymaster General's records (PMG 48), and usually give the recipient's address. There are also registers of deceased pensioners (1877–1918) and of awards of pension made on the disbandment of the force in this class. Among the Colonial Office records are files on pension options at the time of disbandment, arranged by county (CO 904/175–6).

For the earlier force a list of superannuations awarded was published by order of Parliament in 1832, giving names, period of service, amount granted, and the nature of the injury which was the cause of the superannuation.

There are more records relating to the activities of the Irish police, but although there are references among them to individual officers you have no way of finding them short of reading through great numbers of files (CO 903, CO 906, HO 45, HO 100, T 1, T 160–T 164, T 192).

Bibliography

Published Finding Aids

House of Commons Sessional Papers, 1831–1832, vol. XXVI, p. 465 (List of superannuations)

Records

Colonial Office
CO 903   Ireland, Confidential Print, 1885–1919
CO 904   Dublin Castle Records, 1795–1926
CO 906   Irish Office, 1796–1924

Home Office
HO 45   Registered Papers, 1939–1948
HO 100   Ireland, Correspondence and Papers, 1782–1851
HO 184   Royal Irish Constabulary, 1816–1922

Paymaster General's Office
PMG 48   Royal Irish Constabulary, Pensions, 1873–1925

Treasury
T 1   Treasury Board Papers, 1557–1920
T 160   Finance Files, 1887–1948
T 161   Supply Files, 1905–1961
T 162   Establishment Files, 1890–1948
T 163   General Files, 1888–1948
T 164   Pensions (Superannuation Files), 1893–1948
T 192   Ireland Files, 1920–1922

6 Merchant Seamen

There is a wealth of material documenting merchant seamen in the PRO, but it relates mainly to the years 1835 to 1857. There is little from before this period, and after 1857 the surviving records have become scattered.

a Seamen's Registers, 1835–1857

The Merchant Shipping Act of 1835 provided for the registration of seamen. The resulting registers give the name of the seaman, his age, place of birth, rank and the name of his ship, and from 1844 such additional details as a physical description and his service record. Errors in transcription are frequent in the early registers, as many of the entries were made from the scrawled signature of illiterates. It was, moreover, not uncommon for a seaman to give a false name.

The registers are in four separate series, which overlap to some extent and represent different systems of registration. The first series (BT 120) consists simply of alphabetically arranged entries, while the second (BT 119) is roughly alphabetical with an index and cross references to the Crew Lists (see below). A ticket system was introduced in 1845, which lasted until 1853, and the register (BT 113) gives full genealogical details as well as a physical description and a man's service record. The last series (BT 116) after the ticket system was abolished, lists seamen alphabetically, giving age, place of birth, and details of the voyage.

b Muster Rolls, Agreements and Crew Lists

i 1747–1834

A few muster rolls survive for some ports, arranged by year and port, but without indexes (BT 98).

ii 1835–1844

In 1835, Crew Lists replaced the Muster Rolls, and the Registers (above) are the means of reference to them. You will need to look first, therefore, in the Register where you will find the number of the port and the name of the ship. Each port was assigned its own number (there is a key in the class list) and the Crew Lists are arranged by those numbers and by year. There are also Port Rotation Numbers, but there is no longer a key to them so they should be ignored. The Crew Lists (BT 98) should tell you a man's name, age, place of birth, quality (i.e. rank), the ship in which he last served, the date and place of his joining, the time and place of his death or of leaving the ship, and how he was disposed of.

iii 1845–1856

The information in the Crew Lists (BT 98) for these years is like that for the previous period, but the task of locating an entry is much more complicated. Reference is again from the Seamen's Registers (above) but the ship's name is not quoted. C T and M J Watts in their article give a sample entry to illustrate the procedure, for one James Watts in 1846 (BT 113/24):

Out	Home
1140–75–2	1140–75–2
75–6–4	64–31–7

This means that Watts was on a Newcastle registered vessel (75 in the top line), which left Newcastle (75 on the bottom line under 'Out'), on 6 April 1846 (6–4 on the bottom line). He left the ship in London (64 in bottom line under 'Home') on 31 July 1846. The Crew Lists for this period are listed by port and year and, as the ship's name is not known, you must be prepared to search through all the boxes for the appropriate port and year; there may be as many as thirty.

iv 1857–1860
In 1857 the system changed again, and the Crew Lists (BT 98) are arranged thereafter by year and numerically by ship's number. Each ship has a unique number, which can be found in the *Mercantile Navy List.*

v 1861–1938
The PRO holds only a 10% sample of Crew Lists after 1861 (BT 99, BT 100, BT 144, BT 165). The largest single collection of them is now held by the Memorial University of Newfoundland (c. 70%), to which there is a microfiche index in the PRO. A small selection of lists for the period 1861–1913 has been deposited locally, and there is a list of these places of deposit in the class list. The National Maritime Museum has the 90% not held by the PRO for the years 1861, 1862, 1865, 1875, 1885, 1895 and 1905.

c Certificates of Competency and Service: Masters, Mates and Engineers
By an order of 1845, the Board of Trade authorised a system of voluntary examinations of competency for men intending to become masters or mates of foreign going and Home Trade British merchant ships (BT 122–BT 127). These gradually became compulsory. From 1862 there are also certificates for engineers (BT 139–BT 142), and for skippers and mates of fishing boats from 1883 (BT 129, BT 130, BT 138). Colonial certificates were entered separately (BT 128). You should find in the certificates name, place and date of birth, date and place of issue of the certificate and rank examined or served in. Deaths, injuries and retirements have also been noted down.

d Apprentices
An index was formed of all indentured apprentices under the Merchant Shipping Act of 1835, and is now in the PRO (BT 150). In addition, five yearly specimens of the copy indentures of apprentices on merchant vessels and on fishing vessels have been preserved (BT 151, BT 152).

e Births, Deaths and Marriages
By the Seamen's Fund Winding-up Act, 1851, the masters of British ships were required to hand over the wages and effects of any seaman who had died during a voyage. Registers (BT 153) were maintained and provide useful information: the name, Register Ticket number, date of engagement, and the place, date and cause of the man's death, with the name and port of his ship, the master's name, the date and place of payment of the wages, the amount of wages and the date they were sent to the Board of Trade. The indexes to these registers (BT 154, BT 155), by seamen and by ship, give simple page references. Associated with the registers are printed monthly lists of dead seamen (BT 156) giving name and age, rating, nationality or birthplace, last address, and cause and place of death. There are also nine manuscript registers (BT 157), containing half yearly lists of deaths, classified by cause.

Following the Merchant Shipping Act of 1854, registers were compiled from the official logs, of births, marriages and deaths at sea. All three are recorded from 1854 to 1883, births and deaths only from 1883 to 1887, and deaths only from 1888 (BT 158). Masters were further required by the Registration of Births and Deaths Act, 1874, to report births and deaths on board ships to the Registrar General of Shipping and Seamen, where they were entered in two separate registers (BT 159, BT 160).

For further biographical information on ordinary seamen after 1870 and on officers after 1913, you should write to the Registrar General of Shipping and Seamen.

Bibliography

Books

N G Cox, 'The Records of the Registrar General of Shipping and Seamen', *Maritime History*, vol. II (1972), pp. 168–188.
K Matthews, 'Crew Lists, Agreements and Official Logs of the British Empire 1863–1913, now in the possession of the Maritime History Group, Memorial University, Newfoundland', *Business History*, vol. XVI (1974), pp. 78–80
C T and M J Watts, 'Unravelling Merchant Seamen's Records', *Genealogists' Magazine*, vol. XIX (1979), pp. 313–321

Published Finding Aids

Index to the Crew Lists, Agreements and Official Logs at the Memorial University of Newfoundland, microfiche
Mercantile Navy List (London, annually from 1857)

Unpublished Finding Aids
Records of the Registrar General of Shipping and Seamen, PRO leaflet no. 8

Records

Board of Trade: Registrar General of Shipping and Seamen
BT 98   Agreements and Crew Lists, Series I, 1747–1860
BT 99   Agreements and Crew Lists, Series II, 1861–1913
BT 100   Agreements and Crew Lists, Series III, 1835–1954
BT 112   Register of Seamen, Series II, 1835–1844 (index in BT 119)
BT 113   Register of Seamen's Tickets, 1845–1954 (index in BT 114)
BT 114   Alphabetical Register of Seamen's Tickets, 1845–1954 (index to BT 113)
BT 115   Alphabetical Register of Masters, 1845–1954
BT 116   Register of Seamen, Series III, 1853–1857
BT 119   Alphabetical List of Seamen, 1835–1844 (index to BT 112)
BT 120   Register of Seamen, Series I, 1835–1836
BT 122   Registers of Certificates of Competency, Masters and Mates, Foreign Trade, 1845–1900 (index in BT 127)

BT 123	Registers of Certificates of Competency, Masters and Mates of Steamships, 1881–1895 (index in BT 127)
BT 124	Registers of Certificates of Service, Masters and Mates, Foreign Trade, 1850–1888 (index in BT 127)
BT 125	Registers of Certificates of Competency, Masters and Mates, Home Trade, 1854–1888 (index in BT 127)
BT 126	Registers of Certificates of Service, Masters and Mates, Home Trade, 1854–1888 (index in BT 127)
BT 127	Indexes to Registers of Competency and Service, Masters and Mates, Foreign and Home Trade, 1845–1894 (BT 122–BT 126)
BT 128	Registers of Certificates of Competency, Masters and Mates, Colonial Trade, 1871–1921
BT 129	Registers of Certificates of Competency, Skippers, Mates, etc. of Fishing Boats, 1880–1898 (index in BT 138)
BT 130	Registers of Certificates of Service, Skippers, Mates, etc. of Fishing Boats, 1883–1917 (index in BT 138)
BT 138	Indexes to Registers of Competency and Service, Skippers, Mates, etc. of Fishing Boats, 1880–1917 (BT 129, BT 130)
BT 139	Registers of Certificates of Competency, Engineers, 1861–1907 (index in BT 141)
BT 140	Registers of Certificates of Competency, Engineers (Colonial), 1862–1921 (index in BT 141)
BT 141	Indexes to Registers of Certificates of Competency, Engineers, 1861–1921 (BT 139, BT 140)
BT 142	Registers of Certificates of Service, Engineers, 1862–1921
BT 143	Registers of Certificates of Competency and Service, Miscellaneous, 1845–1849
BT 144	Agreements and Crew Lists, Series IV, Fishing Agreements, 1884–1913
BT 150	Index of Apprentices, 1824–1953
BT 151	Apprentices' Indentures, 1845–1950
BT 152	Apprentices' Indentures for Fishing, 1895–1935
BT 153	Registers of Wages and Effects of Deceased Seamen, 1852–1889 (index in BT 154, BT 155)
BT 154	Indexes to Names of Seamen, 1855–1889 (BT 153)
BT 155	Indexes to Names of Ships, 1855–1889 (BT 153)
BT 156	Monthly lists of Deaths of Seamen, 1886–1890
BT 157	Registers of Seamen's Deaths, Classified by Cause, 1882–1888
BT 158	Registers of Births, Deaths and Marriages of Passengers at Sea, 1854–1890
BT 159	Registers of Deaths at Sea of British Nationals, 1875–1888
BT 160	Registers of Births at Sea of British Nationals, 1875–1891
BT 165	Ships' Official Logs, 1902–1912

7 Crown Employees and Civil Servants

There are numerous places among the Public Records to look for material relating to Crown and Public Servants, most notably among the records of the relevant departments of state, but also in other less obvious classes. It would, however, be impractical to attempt to list all the possible places in the PRO where a search might be profitable. Before embarking upon such a search, you should look through the many published lists of officials and the published indexes and calendars, such as that for the Patent Rolls if the office holder in question had a patent of appointment.

For civil servants appointed after 1855, you should write to the Civil Service Department.

Bibliography

Books

G E Aylmer, *The King's Servants, 1625–1642* (London, 1961)
G E Aylmer, *The State's Servants, 1649–1660* (London, 1973)
Guide to the Contents of the Public Record Office (London, 1963, 1968)

Published Finding Aids

An Account of the Commissioners of Customs (1642–1909), Excise (1643–1848), Excise and Hearthmoney (1684–1689), Inland Revenue (1849–1909), and Customs and Excise (1909–1913), (London, 1913)
Calendar of Patent Rolls, Henry III to Elizabeth I (London, 1901–1979)
Calendar of State Papers, Colonial, 1513–1738 (London, 1860–1970)
Calendar of State Papers, Domestic, 1547–1704 (London, 1856–1972)
Calendars of Treasury Books and Papers, 1557–1745 (London, 1868–1962)
Chronological List of Lord High Treasurers and Chief Commissioners of the Treasury, from temp. Henry VII, Appendix to the *25th Report of the Deputy Keeper of the Public Records* (London, 1864)
Colonial Office List (London, annually from 1862)
Court and City Register (London, 1742–1808)
Foreign Office List (London, annually from 1852)
Her Majesty's Letters Patent appointing Commissioners for managing, etc. the Revenue of Customs, 1671–1895 (London, 1897)
The British Imperial Calendar (London, 1810–1872, superseded by the *Civil Service Year Book* from 1873)
List of Sheriffs for England and Wales from the Earliest Times to A. D. 1831, PRO Lists and Indexes, vol. IX (1898)
The Royal Kalendar (London, 1767–1850)
J C Sainty (vols. I–VI), and J M Collinge (vols. VII–VIII), *Office Holders in Modern Britain*, vol. I, *Treasury Officials, 1660–1870*, vol. II, *Officials of the Secretaries of State, 1660–1782*, vol. III, *Officials of the Board of Trade, 1660–1870*, vol. IV, *Admiralty Officials, 1660–1870*, vol. V, *Home Office Officials, 1782–1870*, vol. VI, *Colonial Office Officials, 1794–1870*, vol. VII, *Navy Board Officials, 1660–1832*, vol. VIII, *Foreign Office Officials, 1782–1870* (London, 1972–1979)

Exchequer Officials, Edward I to George III MS
Justices of the Peace, 1642–1700 MS

Records (selection)

Chancery
C 213   Association Oath Rolls, 8 William III

Board of Customs and Excise
CUST 47   Minute Books, 1695–1867
CUST 48   Entry Books of Correspondence, 1668–1839

Lord Chamberlain's Department
LC 3   Registers of the Royal Household, 1641–1902

Lord Steward's Department
LS 13   Miscellaneous Books, 1598–1870 (see LS 13/195)

Paymaster General's Office
PMG 50   Probate Registers, 1836–1915

Public Record Office
PRO 30/19   Chapels Royal Register, 1755–1880

General Register Office
RG 8   Registers, Unauthenticated, Miscellaneous, 1646–1951 (see RG
8/76–78)

8 Welshmen

The high incidence of common surnames and the use of patronymics make Welsh
genealogy difficult. You may be able to obtain help from the Honourable Society
of Cymmrodorion, and for births, marriages and deaths from 1837 you can go to
St Catherine's House (see III/1 above). The National Library of Wales holds
many parish registers and transcripts as well as wills, tithe records and personal
and estate papers.

The three chief groups of records relevant to Welsh genealogy in the PRO are the
census returns (see III/2 above), Non-parochial Registers (III/1) and wills (III/3).

Bibliography

F Jones, 'An Approach to Welsh Genealogy,' *Transactions of the Honorable Society
of Cymmrodorion*, Session 1948, pp. 303–466 (1949)
Guide to Genealogical sources at the National Library of Wales, National Library of
Wales leaflet

9 Irishmen

So many Irish records have been lost or destroyed that it is well worth making a
preliminary approach to the Irish Genealogical Society for help.

The registration of births, marriages and deaths started on 1 January 1864. The records for the whole of Ireland until 1921, for Eire to date, and of Roman Catholic marriages from 1 April 1845 are in the custody of the Registrar General in Dublin, as are the surviving parish registers of the Church of Ireland. Roman Catholic registers seldom pre-date 1820. Unfortunately, the census returns for Ireland have not survived, except for the 1901 and 1911 Censuses, and most Irish wills were destroyed by fire, although seventy two volumes of will books are preserved in the Irish Record Office. For records of land holding you should try the Registry of Deeds in Dublin.

The records of births, marriages and deaths in Northern Ireland since 1 January 1922 are with the Registrar General in Belfast. Many Presbyterian registers are still with the congregation, while others are held by the Presbyterian Historical Society in Belfast. The Public Record Office of Northern Ireland has copies and extracts of many Ulster wills, and for a fee, the Ulster Scot Historical Foundation, at the same address, will undertake genealogical searches.

There are some records in the PRO which may be useful. These include the wills of Irishmen who died with goods in England (see III/3 above), the records of the Irish Tontines of 1773, 1775 and 1777, which cover the years 1773–1871 (see III/9 above and RG 4) and the Civil List establishment for Ireland, 1709–1715 (E 403). Records relating to Irishmen in the Army are plentiful (see IV/1). There were a great number of Irishmen in the Navy (see IV/2).

Bibliography

R ffolliott, *Simple Guide to Irish Genealogy* (London, 1966)

Records

Exchequer
E 403   Enrolments and Registers of Issues, Henry III to 1834 (see E 403/2387, Civil List Establishment, Ireland, 1709–1715)
National Debt Office
NDO 3   Irish Tontines, 1773–1871

10 Scotsmen

Civil registration started in Scotland on 1 January 1855. The records, along with many parish registers (c. 1700–1855) and census returns for 1841–1891 (every ten years) are held by the Registrar General in Edinburgh. You will find wills, judicial records, deeds, etc. in the Scottish Record Office. If you want help, you should get in touch with either the Scottish Genealogy Society or the Scots Ancestry Research Society, and for information about clans try the Scottish Tartans Society.

The PRO has the wills of Scotsmen possessed of property in the form of goods, money and investments in England (see III/3 above), and also the records of the Scottish Church in England (see III/1 above and RG 4).

Bibliography

G H Edwards, *In Search of Scottish Ancestry* (London, 1966)

Published Finding Aids

National Index of Parish Registers, vol. 2, *Sources for Scottish Genealogy and Family History*, ed. D J Steel (London, 1970)
M Stuart, *Scottish Family Histories held in Scottish Libraries* (Edinburgh, 1960)

Records

General Register Office
RG 4   Registers, Authenticated, 1567–1858

11 Manxmen (Isle of Man)

The registration of marriages on the Isle of Man started in 1849, and of births and deaths in 1878. The records are held by the island's General Registry, and searches of them will be made by that office for a fee. You can also obtain information about wills from the Registry, but all other records are kept in the Manx Museum Library.

The only separate records in the PRO are lists of charitable Manx bequests (HO 99).

Records

Home Office
HO 99   Channel Islands etc., Entry Books, 1760–1921 (see HO 99/22)

12 Channel Islanders

Civil registration of births and deaths in the Channel Islands started in 1840, that of marriages in 1919. For these records and for probate records you should apply to the Judicial Greffe on Jersey or the Greffe on Guernsey.

Bibliography

L R Burnes, 'Genealogical Research in the Channel Isles', *Genealogists' Magazine*, vol. XIX, pp. 169–172

13 Protestant Nonconformists

Any extant nonconformist registers (of baptisms, burials and some marriages) are either in the PRO or with the congregation (see III/1, above). If you are looking for nonconformist clergy, the index at Dr Williams' Library should be helpful, and you will find there, in addition, an excellent collection of other material relating to nonconformist history in general.

For help on specific nonconformist sects, you would be well advised to write to the relevant central office. The Quakers (Society of Friends), for example, have a library in London with particularly comprehensive and well kept records, of which many are in print. They also have the indexes to the Quaker registers in the PRO (RG 6). The PRO has rolls of Quaker attornies for the period 1831–1835 (E 3) and 1835–1842 (CP 10). Indexes to the Exchequer rolls are found by reference to the Catalogue of Lists and Indexes, Exchequer.

The Baptists and Presbyterians both have historical societies, and the John Rylands Library in Manchester has records relating to the Unitarians and Presbyterians. The records of the central registry of London Independents, Presbyterians and Baptists, 1742–1837, are in the PRO (Dr Williams' collection, RG 4, original certificates in RG 5). The Methodists (Wesleyans) have their own archival collection in Manchester. The registers of the Wesleyan Metropolitan Registry at Paternoster Row (baptisms in England and Wales, 1808–1888) are in the PRO (RG 4). You should bear in mind that the early followers of Wesley will appear in the parish registers of the established Church.

The PRO has the enrolments of nonconformist trust deeds from 1736 (C 54).

Bibliography

Books

H G Tibbutt, 'Sources for Congregational Church Records', *Transactions of the Congregational History Society*, XIX (1960–1964), pp. 147–155, 230–236
E Welsh, 'The Early Methodists and their Records', *Journal of the Society of Archivists*, IV (1971), p. 210.

Unpublished Finding Aids

Catalogue of Lists and Indexes, Exchequer, TS

Records

Chancery
C 54   Close Rolls
Common Pleas
CP 10   Oath Rolls, 1779–1847
Exchequer
E 3   Attorneys' Oath Rolls, 1830–1875
General Register Office
RG 4   Registers, Authenticated, 1567–1858, including Dr Williams' Registry
(RG 4/4658–4676); Paternoster Row Registry (RG 4/4680 (index),
4677–4679).

14 Roman Catholics

The registers of Catholic churches are either in the PRO (see III/1 above) or with the congregation. If you need help in tracing Catholic ancestors, you should try the Catholic Record Society, the relevant diocesan archivist or the Catholic Central Library. Burials of Catholics often took place in the parish churchyard and the records are, therefore, in the parish registers. An index of Catholic marriages in England is being compiled by Fr. Godfrey Anstruther, O.P.

Records of Catholics in the PRO are largely the records of their persecution, and their bulk accordingly varies with fluctuations in anti-popery. The Recusant Rolls (E 376 and E 377) are annual returns of dissenters (Protestant and Catholic) who had their property forfeit or were fined, 1592–1691. They are the major offenders. You will find a lot on the persecutions in county record offices. Most Catholics supported the King in the Civil War, so their estates may be referred to in *Calendars of the Committee for Compounding with Delinquents*. There are many inventories of Catholic possessions in the State Papers for the Interregnum (SP 28). From the reign of George I and the Jacobite risings, there are lists of papists who forfeited their estates (E 174, KB 18, FEC 1). From this period Catholic wills were enrolled on the Recovery Rolls of the Court of Common Pleas (CP 43). There are lists of Catholic attornies for the period 1830–1875 (E 3) and 1790–1836 (CP 10). Indexes to the former may be found in the Catalogue of Lists and Indexes, Exchequer.

Bibliography

Books

Biographical Studies, vols. I–III, changed to *Recusant History*, from vol. IV, the Journal of the Catholic Record Society (Bognor Regis, 1951 to date)
Catholic Directory (London, annually from 1837)
Catholic Record Society, publications (1905–1979)

Unpublished Finding Aids

Catalogue of Lists and Indexes, CP and KB, TS
Catalogue of Lists and Indexes, Exchequer, TS

Published Finding Aids

Calendar of State Papers, Domestic, Committee for Compounding with Delinquents, 1643–1660 (London, 1889–1893)
Sources for the history of Roman Catholics in England, ed. J H Pollen, SPCK Helps for Students of History, no. 39

Records

Court of Common Pleas
CP 10   Attorney's Oath Rolls, 1790–1836
CP 43   Recovery Rolls, 25 Elizabeth I to 1837 (indexes in IND 16943–9, 17183–17216)

Exchequer

E 3   Exchequer of Pleas, Attorneys' Oath Rolls, 1830–1872
E 174   Returns of Papists' Estates, George I
E 376   Pipe Office, Recusant Rolls Chancellor's Series, 34 Elizabeth I to 1 and
        2 William and Mary
E 377   Pipe Office, Recusant Rolls, Clerk of the Pipe, 34 Elizabeth I to 1 and 2
        William and Mary

Forfeited Estates Commission

FEC 1   Papers, 1552–1744 (Returns of Papists' estates following the 1715
        rebellion cf. E 174)

Court of King's Bench

KB 18   Returns of Papists in Lancaster, George I

State Paper Office

SP 28   Commonwealth Exchequer Papers, 1642–1660 (see SP 28/217A and B)

15 Foreigners in Britain

The records of naturalisations and denizations are kept in the PRO (HO 1–HO 3,
HO 5), but the majority of aliens settling in Britain did not go through the legal
formalities and so do not appear. Indexes have been published for the period
1603–1935.

For immigrants between 1878 and 1960, arriving from places outside Europe by
sea, the Passenger Lists are an additional source of information (BT 26). You will
find name, age, occupation and address in the United Kingdom, and date of
entry into the country but no indication of the intended length of stay. After
1906 the Registers of Passenger Lists (BT 32) give, under the different ports,
the names of the ships and the date of arrival. The Passenger Lists have not been
preserved after 1960, and there are none for arrivals by air.

The registers of some 'foreign' churches in England, in particular refugee
churches (RG 4), and the church of the Russian Orthodox community in London
(RG 8), are in the PRO. Another source is the records of annuities and pensions
paid to refugees for services to the Crown among the Treasury Papers and
Paymaster General's Papers. These include, for instance, allowances to Polish
refugees, 1828–1856, Spaniards, 1855–1909, Frenchmen 1793–1831, American
loyalist pensions, 1780–1835 and accounts concerning refugees from Corsica,
Malta, Holland and Santo Domingo (PMG 53, T 1, T 50, T 93). An important
group of refugees was that of the exiles from the Palatinate, shipped from
Holland to England in 1709, many of whom remained in England rather than
continuing to the New World. There are embarkation lists, received by the
British resident in the Hague, of those leaving Holland, now among the Treasury
files (T 1). There are references to them also in the State Papers (SP 84) and the
Colonial Office records (CO 388), and you can find many wills of bi-national
Dutchmen in the records of the PCC (see III/3 above).

You will find a large number of early references to aliens resident in England in the Chancery and Exchequer records, concerning, for example, alien clergy, foreign merchants, and alien priories (C 47, C 54, C 65, C 66, E 106).

If you have any enquiries about recent naturalisation, you should write to the Home Office.

a Huguenots

Huguenots were French protestants fleeing from religious persecution from the 1550s onwards, and in large numbers after the Revocation of the Edict of Nantes (which had granted toleration to them) in 1685. It is quite possible, however, for a Huguenot ancestor to appear in this country some time after this, as many fled first to Holland or Germany and only later moved to England. If you think this might be the case, you should get in touch with the Huguenot Society of Germany, or the Central Bureau for Genealogy of Holland. There are often strong family traditions of Huguenot descent, and names are usually a good indication of such a background.

The main Huguenot settlements were in London, Norwich, Canterbury, Southampton, Rye, Sandwich, Colchester, Bristol, Plymouth, Thorney and various places in Ireland. There are no known records of any communities which may have existed in the Midlands or the North of England, and there is little on settlement in Scotland. It is, naturally, more difficult to trace a family which struck out on its own to a new part of the country, where no French church existed and they used the local parish church for baptisms. Huguenot burial records are rare at all times, and by the nineteenth century almost non-existent, except for the records of deaths of the inmates of the London Huguenot Hospital, which are in the Huguenot Library.

A great deal has been published by the Huguenot Society of London, and you should start by looking at that readily available material. There is a Huguenot Library in London, which you can use by arrangement with the Honorary Librarian. The staff will undertake a brief search for you, for a fee. You will also find Huguenot material in other areas where they settled, in the Cathedral Library at Canterbury, the County Record Office at Norwich and the City Record Office at Southampton, for instance.

Most of the sources for Huguenot genealogy in the PRO have been included in Huguenot Society publications in some form. The published *Calendars of State Papers* are also useful as are the various lists in print, of aliens resident in England, naturalised, or taking oaths of allegiance (Compiled from the record classes E 169, E 179, E 196, KB 24, RG 4, SP 10–SP 12, SP 44).

b French Emigrés

A French sounding name can also be the result of descent from refugees from the Revolution. There are many letters and papers concerning such people among

Home Office (HO 69), Privy Council (PC 1), Foreign Office (FO 95) and War Office papers (WO 1), from 1789 to 1814. In addition, the Treasury had a French Refugees Relief Committee, 1792–1828 (T 50, T 93), the records of which give names of people receiving pensions.

c Jews

There were Jews in England in the early Middle Ages but descent from members of this early community is virtually impossible to trace. There has been regular Jewish immigration since the seventeenth century, and a steady rate of assimilation into the gentile population, so you may well find a Jewish element in your ancestry. The immigrants were of two sorts: Sephardic (Portuguese, Spanish and Italian), arriving from 1657 onwards; and Ashkenazi (German and East European). The first Ashkenazi came in the 1680s from Holland and Bohemia, but the main influx was of Russians and Poles in the last three decades of the nineteenth century, many of whom were in the clothing trade. You can usually tell which sort of Jew your ancestor was from his name.

The registers of the London Sephardic Synagogue (established in 1701) are in Portuguese, and are partly published. The registers of the Ashkenazi are in Yiddish before 1840, and are not very easily accessible as they are mostly held by the congregations concerned. Many of them, however, are included in the Computer File Index compiled by the Church of Jesus Christ of Latter Day Saints (see III/1 above), and this may well be the best place to start, having traced the family as far as possible through the registers of births, marriages and deaths at St Catherine's House (III/1 above). You can find the names and addresses of synagogues in the Jewish Year Book, and for help on London Ashkenazi Jewry from Rev. J Sunshine in the Offices of the United Synagogue. There are records there of the three old London synagogues from 1709, and they will search these for a fee. You should write for help on the London Sephardic community to the Honorary Genealogist at the Spanish and Portuguese Synagogue where the records are kept. The Jewish Museum is in the same building as the United Synagogue, and contains an invaluable collection of Jewish pedigrees compiled by Sir Thomas Colyer Fergusson.

The most productive sources for specifically Jewish genealogy at the PRO are wills, naturalisation papers and records of change of name. There is a sizeable collection of pre-1858 Jewish wills (about 5% of the Jewish population made wills, and all of them were proved in the PCC; see III/3 above), and they can be most informative as Jewish assets were often in the form of cash and chattels because they were banned from legal landownership. For naturalisation see above in this section, and for change of name, which was quite usual for Jewish immigrants because of persecution see III/4 above.

If you would like to find more Jewish material, there are excellent collections in the Weiner Library (sources for refugees from Nazi Germany) and the Mocatta Library.

Bibliography

Books

Anglo-Jewish Bibliography, *1937–1970*, ed. R P Lehmann (London, 1973)

Anglo-Jewish Notabilities, their Arms and Testamentary Dispositions (Jewish Historical Society of England, London, 1949)

Magna Bibliotheca Anglo-Judaica, ed. C Roth (London, 1937)

J M Ross, 'Naturalisation of Jews in Britain', *Transactions of the Jewish Historical Society of England*, vol. 24 (1975), pp. 59–72

W S Samuel, 'Sources of Anglo-Jewish Genealogy', *Genealogists' Magazine*, vol. VI (1932), pp. 146–159

E R Samuel, 'Jewish Ancestors and where to find them', *Genealogists' Magazine*, vol. XI (1953), pp. 414–441

Published Finding Aids

Bevis Marks Records, Registers of the London Sephardic Synagogue (Oxford, 1940–1949)

Calendar of Close Rolls, 1227–1509 (London, 1892–1963)

Calendar of Patent Rolls, 1216–1575 (London, 1894–1974)

Calendar of State Papers, Domestic Series, 1547–1702 (London, 1856–1972)

Calendar of Treasury Papers, 1557–1728 (London 1868–1889)

Home Office Certificates of Naturalisation, Index, 1844–1935 (London, 1908–1937)

The Jewish Yearbook (London, annually from 1896)

R E G Kirk, *Returns of Aliens in London, 1523–1603* (Huguenot Society, Vol. X, London, 1900–1908)

W A Knittle, *Early Eighteenth Century Palatine Emigration* (Philadelphia, 1937)

List of Jewish persons endenizenised and naturalised, 1609–1799, ed. R D Barnett and A J Diamond (Jewish Historical Society of England, London, 1970)

L D MacWethy, *The Book of Names especially relating to the early Palatines and the First Settlers in the Mohawk Valley* (New York, 1933)

National Index of Parish Registers, vol. III, *Sources for Roman Catholic and Jewish Genealogy and Family History*, ed. D Steel and E R Samuel (London, 1974)

New York Genealogical and Biographical Records, vols. XL and XLI (New York, 1909–1910)

W Page, *Denization and Naturalisation of Aliens in England 1509–1603* (Huguenot Society Publications, vol. VIII, Lymington, 1893)

Registers of Churches, of Huguenots in London and elsewhere, (Huguenot Society, London, 1891–1956)

Rotuli Parliamentorum, Edward I to Henry VII (London, 1783, Index, London, 1832)

W A Shaw, *Letters of Denization and Acts of Naturalisation for Aliens in England, 1603–1800* (Huguenot Society, Lymington, 1911, Manchester, 1923 and London, 1932)

Unpublished Finding Aids

Immigrants: Documents in the Public Record Office, PRO leaflet no. 6

Index to Denizations, 1801–1873, and to Acts of Naturalisation, 1801–1835, TS

Indexes of 'Foreign' Churches, MS
Index of Memorials for Denizations and Naturalisations, 1835–1844, MS
List of papers on French emigrés, TS

Records

Board of Trade
BT 26   Passenger Lists, Inwards, 1878–1960
BT 32   Registers of Passenger Lists, 1906–1951

Chancery
C 47   Miscellanea, Bundle 13, foreign merchants, Henry III to Henry VIII;
        15–21, alien clergy, John to William and Mary
C 54   Close Rolls, 6 John to 1903 (containing enrolments of naturalisation
        certificates, 1844–1873)
C 65   Parliament Rolls, 1 Edward III to 3 and 4 Elizabeth II
C 66   Patent Rolls, 3 John to 9 George VI

Colonial Office
CO 388 Board of Trade, Original Correspondence, 1654–1792

Exchequer
E 106   Extents of Alien Priories, etc., 22 Edward I to 22 Edward IV
E 169   Oaths of Allegiance, etc., 1709–1868
E 179   Subsidy Rolls Henry VIII to William and Mary (for lists of foreigners in
        London, 1423–1581)
E 196   Sacrament Certificates, 1700–1827

Foreign Office
FO 95   Miscellanea, 1639–1942

Home Office
HO 1   Denizations and Naturalisations, 1789–1871 (index in HO 5/25–32)
HO 2   Certificates of Aliens, 1836–1852
HO 3   Returns and Papers, 1836–1869
HO 5   Aliens Entry Books, 1794–1921 (index to HO 2, HO 5/25–32)
HO 45   Registered Papers, 1839–1946 (denizations and naturalisations,
        1841–1878, see HO 144)
HO 69   Bouillon Papers, 1789–1809
HO 144 Registered Papers, Supplementary, 1878–1946 (closed for 100 years)

Court of King's Bench
KB 24   Swearing or Oath Rolls, 1673–1906 (published in Huguenot Society,
        vol. XXVII)

Privy Council Office
PC 1   Papers, 1481–1946

Paymaster General's Office
PMG 53   Allowances to Polish Refugees and Distressed Spaniards, 1855–1909

General Register Office
RG 4   Registers, Authenticated, 1567–1858
RG 8   Registers, Unauthenticated, Miscellaneous, 1646–1951

State Paper Office
SP 10   State Papers, Domestic, Edward VI
SP 11   State Papers, Domestic, Mary I
SP 12   State Papers, Domestic, Elizabeth I
SP 44   Entry Books, 1661–1828 (for denizations, 1681–1688 see SP 44/67)
SP 84   State Papers, Foreign, Holland, 1585–1780

Treasury
T 1   Treasury Board Papers, 1557–1920 (for pensions to refugees)
T 50   Documents relating to Refugees, 1780–1856
T 93   French Refugees' Relief Committee, 1792–1828

War Office
WO 1   In-Letters, 1732–1868

16 British Nationals Abroad

If you are looking for information concerning someone who served abroad in the
Colonial or Foreign Services, you should look among the relevant records in the
PRO (CO, DO, FO). The records of the Levant Company are among the State
Papers (SP), and those of companies trading to Africa are among the Treasury
records (T). For British nationals abroad, but not necessarily in an official
capacity there are various registers of births, marriages and deaths which may be
helpful. Some of these from British embassies and consulates are among the
Foreign Office records (FO), but most of them were held by the Registrar General
(RG 32–RG 36, RG 43). Most of the foreign registers date from the 1830's, with
the exception of Paris (from 1784), the Hague (from 1627), Rotterdam (from
1708) and Leghorn (from 1707). There are also registers of births, marriages and
deaths at sea (BT 158–BT 160), and some death certificates for France and
Belgium for 1914–1921 (RG 35).

The General Register Office at St Catherine's House has a miscellaneous
collection of indexes and registers of British nationals abroad, including, in
particular, returns from Army Chaplains of births (1760–1955), marriages
(1796–1955) and deaths (1761–1970s), and War deaths, 1914–1921 and
1939–1945. As well as these registers, the General Register Office has an index of
the Foreign Registers at the PRO. Many records of baptisms, marriages and
burials abroad for the years 1706–1939, mainly from Anglican congregations,
are preserved in the Guildhall and Lambeth Palace Libraries.

Births, deaths and marriages at sea were recorded in the ship's log and can only
be found (pre-1837) if the ship's name is known. From 1837 the records are at the
General Register Office in St Catherine's House. From 1854 these are in the
registers in the PRO. The tradition associating baptisms at sea with St Dunstan's,
Stepney, is fallacious (see article by A D Ridge).

The wills of Britons who died abroad were usually proved in the Prerogative
Court of Canterbury, and are thus now in the PRO (see III/3 above).

Bibliography

Abstract of Arrangements respecting Registration of Births, Marriages and Deaths
   (London, 1952)
I A Baxter, *Brief Guide to Biographical Sources in the India Office Library* (London,
   1979)
The Records of the Colonial and Dominions Offices, PRO Handbook No. 3,
   (London, 1964)
The Records of the Foreign Office, 1782–1939, PRO Handbook, No. 13 (London,
   1969)
A D Ridge, 'All at Sea', *Archives*, VI (1964) pp. 229–234

Records

Board of Trade
BT 158   Registers and Indexes of Births, Marriages and Deaths of Passengers at
            Sea, 1854–1890
BT 159   Registers of Deaths at Sea of British Nationals, 1875–1888
BT 160   Registers of Births at Sea of British Nationals, 1875–1891
CO   Colonial Office records
DO   Dominions Office records
FO   Foreign Office records

General Register Office
RG 32   Miscellaneous Foreign Returns, 1831–1946 (index in RG 43)
RG 33   Foreign Registers and Returns, 1627–1958 (index in RG 43)
RG 34   Foreign Marriages, 1826–1921 (index in RG 43)
RG 35   Foreign Deaths, 1830–1921 (index in RG 43)
RG 36   Registers and Returns of Births, Marriages and Deaths in the
            Protectorates, etc. of Africa and Asia, 1895–1945 (index in RG 43)
RG 43   Miscellaneous Foreign Returns of Births, Marriages and Deaths, Indexes,
            1627–1947 (index to RG 32–RG 36)

State Paper Office
SP 110/70   Register of births, marriages and deaths, Aleppo, 1756–1800
               (Levant Company)

Treasury
T 70   African Companies, 1660–1833

17 Emigrants

The PRO has many records relating to emigration but, because of the nature and
limited scope of many of them, there can be no certainty of finding information
on any particular individual.

Passenger Lists are very rare from before 1800, and there was no regular series of
them kept until 1890. Thereafter, you will find them arranged by year under the
names of the ports of departure, and they give name, age, occupation and some
sort of address of the passenger (BT 27). There are Registers of Passenger Lists

(BT 32) which are helpful in indicating the ships leaving each port. Prior to 1920 only the month, not the exact date, of departure is given.

It was not common, before the First World War, for passports to be issued to people travelling abroad. A few were, in particular the Exchequer Licences to Pass Beyond the Seas (E 157) which include lists and registers of soldiers taking the Oath of Allegiance before going to serve in the Low Countries (1613–1624); people going abroad, mainly to Holland (1624–1632); and passengers bound for New England, Barbados, Maryland, Virginia and other colonies (1634–1639 and 1677).* For the period 1795–1948 the Foreign Office Passport Registers (FO 610, FO 611) have entries of names and intended destinations abroad of all applicants for passports, but before 1915 these were almost all for official Foreign Office travel or for people going on the Grand Tour of Europe.

The Treasury (T) handled a considerable volume of colonial business, and you may find useful references in the published calendars, which will lead you to the original books and papers. The Privy Council was also involved, receiving, for example, petitions from colonists, warrants for grants or surrenders of office, instructions to governors and warrants for letters of marque (PC 1, PC 2, PC 5).

Many emigrants had assistance with their passage from the parish under the provisions of the 1834 Poor Law. The records, which are normally lists of emigrants giving occupations and destinations, are arranged by counties and Poor Law Unions, so you will need to know where the emigrant came from (MH 12).

The correspondence of the Colonial Office (CO) contains a class of letters (CO 384) concerning emigration, including letters from settlers or from people hoping to settle in the colonies between 1817 and 1896. You may also find, among other correspondence files, details of land grants and applications for them, although you may have a long search.

There are one or two more places where a very long search, with inadequate finding aids, may be successful. The Admiralty records include, for instance, medical journals from emigrant ships and convict ships (ADM 101); and registers of convicts (ADM 6) and troops (ADM 108, MT 23) shipped to various parts of the world. The Audit Office accounts have references to pensions paid to colonists (AO 1–AO 3), and the Chancery Patent Rolls (C 66) contain entries relating to grants of offices and lands in America and elsewhere.

a North Americans
Owing to the fact that there was no regular series of passenger lists or passports until relatively recently, that there was no central registrations of births, marriages and deaths before 1837 (1855 in Scotland), and that there is no national index of parish registers, you are very unlikely to identify an individual, unless you know the place of origin, if the family emigrated before 1837 (or 1855 from Scotland). The Mormon Computer File Index of baptisms (see III/1 above) may

---

* All indexed by J C Hotten (see bibliography).

be a good place to start if you need to find the place of origin, but your success will depend largely on how common the surname is. It is essential that you should do some preliminary work from published means of reference, and if possible, among records in the U.S.A. or Canada to try to establish at least the port and date of entry.

Among the registers of the Treasury are four volumes (T 47/9–12) which give details of emigrants going from England, Wales and Scotland to the New World between 1773 and 1776. The information in those for England and Wales has been summarised in the card index, which gives name, age, occupation, reason for leaving the country, last place of residence, date of departure, and destination. For the period 1719–1744, the Treasury records also contain Money Warrants (T 53) which include lists of felons transported to the American colonies.

Some information on colonists can be found in the correspondence and papers of the Colonial Office (CO), which cover the West Indies as well as the continent of America, and start in 1574. More detail on tracts of land in West and East New Jersey, Pennsylvania, New England and elsewhere is in the records of the West New Jersey Society (TS 12), a company formed in 1691 for the division of the land. There are many names in the correspondence, minute books, share transfers, deeds and claims. There are records relating to slave owners in the West Indies, 1812–1846 among Treasury, Audit Office and National Debt Office papers (T 71, AO 14, NDO 4).

During and after the American War of Independence, many people suffered losses on account of their loyalty to the British Crown, and were entitled to claim compensation under the Treaty of Peace in 1783 and a new Treaty of Amity between Great Britain and the United States of America in 1794. The Treasury records contain the reports of commissioners investigating individual claims, and some compensation and pension lists, 1780–1835 (T 50, T 79). Commissioners were also appointed by the Exchequer and Audit Department in 1802 (AO 12, AO 13), and their papers contain lists of claimants of pensions, and papers supporting their claims. The Declared Accounts of the Audit Office (AO 1) contain the accounts of payments and pensions made. Similar claims for compensation to loyalists were made when East Florida was ceded to Spain in 1783, and they are now among the Treasury records (T 77).

Americans who died with goods in the United Kingdom had their wills proved in the Prerogative Court of Canterbury, so they are now to be found among the PCC records in the PRO (see III/3 above).

The Genealogical Society of Utah has a huge index containing a great deal of information from British sources, including microfilm copies of the 1841–1871 Census Returns; and photocopies, microfilms and transcripts of much of the PRO's American material can be consulted in the Library of Congress, some state libraries, and the Public Archives of Canada. You can obtain copies of PRO publications from the British Information Services. There are several genealogical societies that may be worth contacting, in particular the National

Genealogical Society in Washington, and the Ontario, British Columbia, Saskatchewan and Alberta Societies.

b Australians and New Zealanders

Until the Passenger Lists begin in 1890 (BT 27) there are few records relating to voluntary emigrants; you will find far more extensive documentation of condemned deportees. The fact that a man's family also travelled to the colony does not mean that he was not a convict, as many 'came free' rather than remain in England.

The principal source for convicts is the series of Transportation Registers (HO 11) which contain lists of convicts carried in the transport ships; each volume has an index of ships' names. In the lists you will find the full names of each convict, the term of his or her transportation, and the date and place of conviction. This last piece of information may enable you to search for further details in the Criminal Registers and the Assize Court records.

The Criminal Registers (HO 26, HO 27), which begin in 1791 for Middlesex and 1805 for all other counties in England and Wales, record the names of all people charged with indictable offences and sometimes give personal details. Assize records (ASSI) can provide details about felons who were sentenced to death on conviction for such crimes as manslaughter, horse-stealing and house-breaking, but were afterwards reprieved and sentenced to transportation. Unless, however, you already have precise information from the Registers on the date and place of conviction, a search of the records of the Assizes would be a daunting task.

A series of censuses of the convict population of New South Wales and Tasmania was made at intervals between 1788 and 1859 (HO 10), which include the names of members of convicts' families, who either 'came free' or were 'born in the colony' as well as the convicts themselves. The census of 1828 is the most complete and thus the most valuable. It contains the names of more than 35,000 people, with their ages, religions, families, residences, occupations and details of stock and land held. In addition there is an indication of whether each person came to the colony free or in bond, or was born in the colony, and of the ship and year of arrival. Some of the earlier censuses also give details of the date and place of trial in England.

Colonial Office (CO) correspondence, entry books and registers contain material which may be of use, including lists of emigrant settlers and convicts, 1801–1821 (CO 201). There are also some useful War Office papers, relating to Army pensioners who were encouraged to emigrate to New South Wales and New Zealand (WO 1, WO 43).

Many of the records of transportation to Australia have been indexed by the Society of Australian Genealogists, who can also offer help and advice. There are microfilms of many PRO records concerning Australia at the National Library in Canberra and the Mitchell Library, Sydney. Genealogists in New Zealand should get in touch with the New Zealand Society of Genealogists.

c South Africans

There is some material in the PRO on settlers and grants of land among the correspondence, entry books and registers of the Colonial Office (CO 48, CO 49, CO 336, CO 462), beginning in 1795. The Genealogical Society of South Africa will give advice.

d The British in India

The records of the British in India, including the registration of baptisms, marriages and burials, and also wills, are preserved among the India Office Records.

Bibliography

Books

I A Baxter, *Brief Guide to Biographical Sources in the India Office Library* (London, 1979)

R H Ellis, 'Records of the American Loyalists' Claims in the Public Record Office', *Genealogists' Magazine*, vol. XII (1958) pp. 375–378, 407–410, 433–435.

H B Guppy, *Homes of Family Names in Great Britain* (Baltimore, 1968)

M and J Kaminkow, *Emigrants in Bondage* (Baltimore, 1967)

The Records of the Colonial and Dominions Offices, PRO Handbook No. 3 (London, 1964)

Published Finding Aids

Acts of the Privy Council of England, Colonial Series, 1613–1783 (London, 1908–1912)

Alphabetical Guide to War Office and other Military Records preserved in the Public Record Office, PRO Lists and Indexes, LIII (London, 1931)

C M Andrews, *Guide to the Materials for American History to 1793 in the Public Record Office of Great Britain* (Washington 1912 and 1914)

C E Banks and E E Brownell, *Topographical Dictionary of 2885 English Emigrants to New England, 1620–1650* (New York, 1963, 1976)

Calendar of State Papers, Colonial, America and West Indies, 1574–1738 (London, 1860–1969)

Calendar of Treasury Books, 1660–1718 (London, 1904–1962)

Calendar of Treasury Papers, 1557–1728 (London, 1868–1889)

Calendar of Treasury Books and Papers, 1729–1745 (London, 1898–1903)

P W Coldham, *English Estates of American Colonists* (Baltimore, 1980), covering 1700–1799

J C Hotten, *Original Lists of Persons emigrating to America, 1600–1700* (London, 1874)

C B Jewson, *Transcript of Three Registers of Passengers from Great Yarmouth to Holland and New England, 1637–1639*, Norfolk Record Society, vol. XXV (1954)

Journals of the Board of Trade and Plantations, 1704–1782 (London, 1920–1938)

J and M Kaminkow, *A List of Emigrants from England to America, 1718–1759* (Baltimore, 1964)

A H Lancour, *A Bibliography of Ships' Passenger Lists, 1538–1825* (New York, 1963)

List of Colonial Office Records, PRO Lists and Indexes, vol. XXXVI (London, 1911)

List of Records of the Treasury, Paymaster General's Office, Exchequer and Audit Department and Board of Trade, prior to 1837, PRO Lists and Indexes No. XLVI (London, 1922)

List of State Papers, Domestic, 1547–1792, and Home Office, Records, 1782–1837, PRO Lists and Indexes, vol. XLIII (London, 1914)

L L Robson, *The Convict Settlers of Australia* (Melbourne, 1965)

Unpublished Finding Aids

Card index to Treasury Registers of emigrants (T 47/9–12)

Indexes to Chancery Patent Rolls, 1 Elizabeth I–22 George V, MS

Index to Colonial Office, New South Wales Original Correspondence, 1823–1833, TS (also available at the Mitchell Library, Sydney and Melbourne Public Library)

Index of Names to American Loyalist Claims (AO 12 and 13), TS

Records

Admiralty

ADM 6   Registers, Returns and Certificates, 1673–1859 (for registers of convicts on ships, 1819–1834)

ADM 101   Medical Journals (include emigrant ships 1815–1853, convict ships, 1817–1853)

ADM 108   Admiralty Transport Department Records, 1773–1837

Exchequer and Audit Office

AO 1   Declared Accounts, 1536–1828

AO 2   Declared and Passed Accounts, 1803–1848

AO 3   Accounts, Various, 1539–1886

AO 12   American Loyalists' Claims, 1776–1831

AO 13   American Loyalists' Claims, 1780–1835

AO 14   Claims Various, 1795–1846

ASSI   Clerks of Assize

Board of Trade

BT 27   Passenger Lists, Outwards, 1890–1960

BT 32   Registers of Passenger Lists, 1906–1951

Chancery

C 66   Patent Rolls, 3 John to 9 George VI

Colonial Office

CO 1   Colonial Papers, General, 1574–1757

CO 5   America, Original Correspondence, 1606–1807

CO 48   Cape of Good Hope, Original Correspondence, 1807–1910

CO 49   Cape of Good Hope, Entry Books, 1795–1872

CO 201   New South Wales, Original Correspondence, 1784–1900

CO 202   New South Wales, Entry Books, 1786–1873
CO 207   Entry Books relating to Convicts (microfilm), 1788–1868
CO 323   Colonies, General, Original Correspondence, 1689–1940
CO 324   Colonies, General, Entry Books, 1662–1872
CO 336   Cape of Good Hope, Registers, 1850–1910
CO 360   New South Wales, Registers, 1849–1900
CO 369   New South Wales, Out Letters, 1873–1900
CO 381   Colonies General, Entry Books, 1740, 1791–1872
CO 384   Emigration, Original Correspondence, 1817–1896
CO 385   Emigration, Entry Books, 1814–1871
CO 386   Land and Emigration Commission, 1833–1894
CO 391   Board of Trade, Minutes, 1675–1782
CO 462   Cape of Good Hope, Register of Out-Letters, 1872–1910

Exchequer
E 157   Licences to Pass Beyond the Seas, Elizabeth I to 1677
E 370   Lord Treasurer's Remembrancer and Pipe Office, Miscellaneous Rolls, Henry II to 1840

Foreign Office
FO 610   Passport Registers, 1795–1943 (index in FO 611)
FO 611   Indexes of Names, 1851–1916

Home Office
HO 10   Convicts, New South Wales and Tasmania, 1788–1859
HO 11   Convict Transportation Registers, 1787–1870
HO 26   Criminal Registers, 1791–1849
HO 27   Criminal Registers, 1805–1892

Ministry of Health
MH 12   Poor Law Union Papers, 1833–1909

Ministry of Transport
MT 23   Admiralty Transport Department, Correspondence and Papers, 1795–1917

National Debt Office
NDO 4   West Indies Slave Compensation, 1835–1842

Privy Council Office
PC 1   Papers, 1481–1946
PC 2   Registers, 1540–1960
PC 5   Plantation Books, 1678–1806

Treasury
T 1   Treasury Board Papers, 1557–1920
T 27   Out letters, General, 1668–1920
T 29   Minute Books, 1667–1870
T 47   Registers, Various (includes registers of emigrants, 1773–1776, T 47/9–12)
T 50   Documents relating to Refugees, 1780–1856
T 52   King's Warrants, 1667–1857
T 53   Warrants relating to Money, 1676–1859
T 54   Warrants not relating to Money, 1667–1849

T 60   Order Books, 1667–1831
T 71   Slave Registration and Compensation, 1812–1846
T 77   East Florida Claims Commission, 1740–1789
T 79   American Loyalist Claims Commission, 1777–1841
T 99   Minute Books, Supplementary, 1690–1691, 1830–1832

Treasury Solicitor's Office
T 12   West New Jersey Society, 1658–1921

War Office
WO 1   In-Letters, 1732–1869 (for emigration of Army pensioners, 1846–1851)
WO 43 Old Series Papers, 1809–1857 (for papers on emigration of poor
       pensioners)

18 Clergymen

There are several published works, in particular *Crockford's* and the lists of
Oxford and Cambridge *Alumni*, which you should first consult for information
about Anglican clergy. Records relating to ordinations will be found in the
appropriate diocesan archive.

The PRO has Clergy Institution Books (E 331), indexed by the name of the
incumbent, for the period 1556–1838, which give the name of the clergyman, his
parish, his patron and the date. The Ecclesiastical Census of 1851 might be worth
consulting (HO 129).

Bibliography

Published Finding Aids

Crockford's Clerical Directory (Oxford, from 1858)
J Foster, *Alumni Oxonienses, 1500–1886* (Oxford, 1891)
J Le Neve, *Fasti Ecclesiae Anglicanae* (London, 1716)
J and J A Venn, *Alumni Cantabrigienses, from the Earliest Times to 1900*
   (Cambridge, 1922–1927)

Unpublished Finding Aids

Institution Books, Indexes, 1556–1838, MS
The Ecclesiastical Census of 1851, PRO leaflet no. 3

Records

Exchequer
E 331   Bishops' Certificates of Institutions to Benefices, 1544–1912
Home Office
HO 129 Census Papers: Ecclesiastical Returns, 1851

V Part of the inventory of the possessions of Thomas Hall, an Eton schoolboy, 11 Oct. 1676
(PROB 4/10015)

**VI Sketches of searchers for wills, in the
Prerogative Office in Doctors' Commons.
Nineteenth century** (PROB 45)

19 Lawyers

From 1775 onwards the easiest means of reference to lawyers is the *Law List*, published every year. Apart from this, for barristers, many of the records of the various Inns of Court have been printed, and the lists of *Alumni* of Oxford and Cambridge should be useful. For attorneys and solicitors practising between 1730 and 1775, you can use the articles of clerkship in the PRO. There is no central index or system for these: the articles of an attorney are found among the records of the court where he was admitted to practise.

For civilian lawyers, i.e. those who practised in the church courts and the High Court of Admiralty, there is a selective card index of advocates and proctors in the PRO. The admission of London proctors (attorneys), namely those practising in Doctors' Commons, was recorded in the Registers of the Archbishop of Canterbury, kept at Lambeth Palace Library. There are short biographies of the London advocates (civilian barristers) in the work by G D Squibb. Records of lawyers who practised in provincial church courts are probably best sought in diocesan and county record offices.

Bibliography

Published Finding Aids

Act Books of the Archbishops of Canterbury, 1663–1859, 2 parts ed. E H W Dunkin, C Jenkins and E A Fry (British Record Society, Index Library, 1929)
Law List (annually from 1775)
List of Attorneys and Solicitors admitted in pursuance of the late Act 1729–1731 (London, 1729–1731)
G D Squibb, *Doctors' Commons* (Oxford, 1977)

Unpublished Finding Aids

Card index to advocates and proctors (available on request)
Records of Attorneys and Solicitors (TS, search rooms)

Records

Chancery
C 217   Petty Bag Office, Miscellaneous Papers, Elizabeth I to 1889

Palatinate of Chester
CHES 36   Attorneys, 1697–1830

Court of Common Pleas
CP 5   Articles of Clerkship, 1730–1838
CP 8   Admission Rolls, 1838–1860
CP 10   Oath Rolls, 1779–1847
CP 11   Rolls of Attorneys, 1730–1750

Palatinate of Durham
DURH 3   Cursitor's Records, 1311–1865 (for Oath Roll of Attorneys,
         1730–1841 and File of Admissions of Attorneys, 1660–1723, DURH
         3/217–218)
DURH 9   Affidavits of Attorneys' Clerks, 1750–1834

Exchequer of Pleas
E 3   Attorneys' Oath Rolls, 1830–1872
E 4   Books of Attorneys, 1830–1855
Exchequer: King's Remembrancer
E 108   Solicitors' Certificate Book 1785–1843
E 200   Solicitors' Oath Roll, 1772–1841

Supreme Court of Judicature
J 8   Articles of Clerkship, 1876–1904
J 9   Affidavits of due execution of Articles of Clerkship, 1875–1903

Court of King's Bench
KB 104   Articles of Clerkship, 1838–1875
KB 105   Affidavits of due execution of Articles of Clerkship, 1775–1817
KB 106   Affidavits of due execution of Articles of Clerkship, 1817–1834
KB 107   Affidavits of due execution of Articles of Clerkship, 1834–1875

Palatinate of Lancaster
PL 23   Articles of Clerkship, 1730–1875

20 Bankrupts

Insolvents who went through the legal procedure of declaring themselves
bankrupt can be found in the *London Gazette*. There are bankruptcy registers of
petitions from 1912 in the Thomas More Buildings of the Royal Courts of
Justice, in which you can have a brief search made for a fee. The PRO holds
records of bankruptcy proceedings (B) for the period 1710–1958, but they are
closed for 75 years.

Bibliography

Published Finding Aids

London Gazette (annually from 1665, originally called the *Oxford Gazette*)

Records

Court of Bankruptcy
B 3   Bankruptcy Commissions Files, 1759–1911

21 Criminals

There is a vast mass of documentation on crime in the PRO but the records are
not easy to handle and the genealogist should be prepared for a long and possibly

unrewarding task. It has frequently been found that newspaper reports of crimes give considerably more detail than can be found in surviving court records.

For petty larceny and breaches of the peace the best place to start looking is in the county record office, among the quarter sessions records, many of which are in print. Minor offences could also be dealt with by the manorial court (see V below).

Of the material in the PRO, the assize records (ASSI) usually provide little genealogical information, except the accused's place of residence, which you will find in the indictment. If depositions happen to survive the names, ages and addresses of the deponents will be given. Unless your period and area are covered by the published calendars, a speculative search is ill advised. The records of the Central Criminal Court at the Old Bailey (which was also the Assize Court for London from 1834) are retained at the court, and may be seen by appointment. There are depositions for the period 1839–1922 in the PRO (CRIM 1), as well as printed copies of proceedings from 1801 to 1904 (PCOM 1), and the Home Office records contain returns made by the Clerk of the Sessions of prisoners committed for trial at the Old Bailey from 1815 to 1849 (HO 16). The records of London sessions for gaol delivery and oyer and terminer before 1834 are in the Corporation of London Record Office; those for Middlesex are in the Greater London Record Office. You may also find the registers and calendars of prisons helpful, and relatively easy to use (HO 26, HO 27, HO 77, HO 140, MEPO 6).

For prisoners deported to the colonies see IV/17 above.

Bibliography

Published Finding Aids

Calendar of Assize Records, Hertfordshire Indictments, Elizabeth I and James I, ed. J S Cockburn (London, 1975)
Calendar of Assize Records, Sussex Indictments, Elizabeth I and James I, ed. J S Cockburn (London, 1975)
Calendar of Assize Records, Essex Indictments, Elizabeth I, ed. J S Cockburn (London, 1978)
Calendar of Assize Records, Kent Indictments, Elizabeth I, ed. J S Cockburn (London, 1979)
Calendar of Assize Records, Surrey Indictments, Elizabeth I, ed. J S Cockburn (London, 1980)

Unpublished Finding Aids

Records of the Clerks of Assize, PRO leaflet No. 29

Records (selection)

ASSI   Clerks of Assize

Central Criminal Court

CRIM 1   Depositions, 1839–1922

DPP   Director of Public Prosecutions, 1846–1952 (closed for 75 years)

Home Office
HO 16   Old Bailey Sessions, 1815–1849
HO 26   Criminal Registers, 1791–1840
HO 27   Criminal Registers, 1805–1892
HO 77   Newgate Calendar, 1782–1853
HO 140   Calendars of Prisoners, 1868–1958

KB   Court of King's Bench

Metropolitan Police
MEPO 6   Habitual Criminals Registers, 1881–1941

Prison Commission
PCOM 1   Sessions Papers, Old Bailey, 1801–1904

PRIS   King's Bench, Fleet and Marshalsea Prisons, 1685–1862

22 Victims of Civil Air Crashes

Records

Ministry of Aviation
AVIA 5   Aircraft Accident Reports, 1919–1936 (for names of pilots, owners and
         passengers)

23 Railwaymen

The records of the railway companies and their staffs before nationalisation are
now in the PRO (RAIL). The volume of documentation, however, varies
considerably from one company to another.

Unpublished Finding Aids

Card index of subjects to British Transport Historical Records

Records

RAIL   British Transport Historical Records

24 Prisoners of War

Most records in the PRO on prisoners of war from before the two World Wars
relate to the expenses of holding foreign prisoners. The exception is a collection
of returns of British prisoners at Lille in 1798 (WO 28).

For the South African War (1899–1902) there are lists of Boer prisoners among
the records of the War Office (WO 108/302–5).

No lists of First World War prisoners (on either side) ever reached the PRO.

For the Second World War there are no nominal lists of prisoners in British hands. For British prisoners you can apply to the International Red Cross who hold lists of prisoners from both World Wars. Narratives of individual escapees are in the PRO, but they are subject to a 75 year closure period (WO 165/39, WO 208/3242–3566). Reports of Red Cross inspections of prison camps (WO 222, WO 224) are available as is material gleaned from contact with prisoners by radio or from escapees (WO 165).

Information about RAF prisoners may be sought in the AIR classes listed below. Particularly useful is a list of air force prisoners in German hands, 1944–45 (AIR 20/2336).

For Prisoners of War at Verdun between 1804 and 1815, there is in France an index of births, marriages and deaths, which can be searched for you for a fee, by Mme M Audin, to whom you should write.

Unpublished Finding Aids

Prisoners of War, PRO leaflet no. 39

Records

Air Ministry

AIR 2   Air Departments Correspondence, (Code B89), 1887–1969

AIR 20   Unregistered Papers, 1912–1961

AIR 40   Directorate of Intelligence, 1923–1947 (prisoners of war, 1897–1911, AIR 40/1544–1552)

Colonial Office

CO 693   Dominions, War of 1914–1918, Prisoners, Original Correspondence, 1917–1919

CO 754   War of 1914–1918, Prisoners, Register of Correspondence, 1914–1919

CO 755   War of 1914–1918, Prisoners, Register of Out-Letters, 1917–1919

Foreign Office

FO 383   General Correspondence, Prisoners, 1915–1919

FO 916   Consular (War) Department, Prisoners of War and Internees, 1940–1946

War Office

WO 28   Headquarters, 1746–1901

WO 108   South African War Papers, 1899–1905

WO 165   War Diaries, Directorates, 1938–1947 (MI 9, WO 165/39; MI 19, WO 165/41)

WO 208   Directorate of Military Intelligence, 1926–1946

WO 222   Medical Historian, 1914–1949

WO 224   Enemy Prisoner of War Camps, Reports of International Red Cross and Protecting Powers, 1941–1947

25 Living Persons

Under some circumstances, the Red Cross and the Salvation Army will undertake to trace people, but this is usually only to mitigate suffering. Family Researchers Ltd. will trace people for a fee. Tracing may also be carried out through the Department of Health and Social Security. You should obtain leaflet PAS. 6 from the General Register Office.

V Pre-parish register genealogy

Before the introduction of parish registers in the middle of the sixteenth century, most people's lives went undocumented. Such records as exist are largely the random survivals of private transactions and the records of litigation and of the sovereign's interference with his subjects. Because of the difficulties of reading and searching medieval records, the genealogist is advised to steer clear of anything that does not have some modern means of reference. It would be senseless for you to plunge into the Plea Rolls of the Court of Common Pleas, for instance.

The standard stock-in-trade of the medieval genealogist are Inquisitions Post Mortem (I.P.M.s), Feet of Fines and the Rolls of various courts. Inquisitions (C 132–C 143, C 145, E 136, E 149–E 152) were inquests concerning the estate of tenants in chief (i.e. tenants holding directly from the Crown) on their death. There are a number of calendars in print, and many also have been published by local record societies. The Feet of Fines (CP 25, DURH 12) are the records of fictitious law suits entered into so as to evade conveyancing restrictions, and they run from 1190 until 1833. Many of these, too, have been printed by local record societies. The indexes to Feet of Fines in the Court of Common Pleas are listed in the *Catalogue of Lists and Indexes*, *KB and CP*.

The best place to look for ordinary, humble folk is on the court roll of the appropriate manor. This gives details of minor offences, and of land held by copyhold from the lord of the manor. You may also find some pedigrees. There are a number of manorial court rolls in the PRO (see the published list), but most are elsewhere, and you should consult the National Register of Archives at the Historical Manuscripts Commission to locate them. For land held freehold there are many thousands of deeds in the PRO, but no central index, so the one in the *Calendar of Ancient Deeds* is valuable (C 146–C 148; see III/7 above).

Medieval genealogy in the PRO is largely a question of looking through the indexes to the various calendars of the rolls of Chancery, Exchequer and King's Bench. The Charter Rolls (C 53), for example, contain grants of land and privileges; the Patent Rolls (C 66) have grants for life, commissions and licences to alienate land; and the back of the Close Rolls (C 54, C 55) were used to enroll all kinds of private deed, including those for sales, leases, enclosure awards, bankrupts' estates, change of name and naturalisation. There are many pedigrees on the Curia Regis (KB 26) and the Plea Rolls (CP 40). You may also find useful the copious extracts, mainly from the De Banco (Plea) Rolls and similar legal records, made by General Plantagenet-Harrison in the late nineteenth century. There are several volumes, all hand-written with indexes, which are on the whole reliable. His main interests were in Yorkshire, and in all pedigrees, but you should be cautious in trusting to the accuracy of the latter.

Tax returns can also be useful; the list of Subsidy Rolls (E 179) indicates where names appear. The Certificates of Residence (E 115) give the names and addresses of many sixteenth and seventeenth century tax payers with a valuation of their property; they were returned by people who were not permanently resident in one place, many because they had two or more homes, so as to avoid being assessed twice.

See also III/3, 6, 7 and 8 above.

Bibliography

Books

M W Beresford, 'Lay Subsidies', I '1290–1334'; II 'after 1334', *Amateur Historian*, vol. III (1958), pp. 325–328, vol. IV (1959), pp. 101–109

M W Beresford, 'Poll Taxes of 1377, 1379 and 1381', *Amateur Historian*, vol. III (1958), pp. 271—278

R F Hunnisett, 'The Reliability of Inquisitions as Historical Evidence', *The Study of Medieval Records*, ed. D A Bullough and R L Storey (Oxford, 1971)

R E Latham, 'Hints on Interpreting the Public Records, III Inquisitions Post Mortem'; 'IV Plea Rolls', *Amateur Historian*, vol. I (1953), pp. 77–81, 155–158

M McGuiness, 'Inquisitions Post Mortem', *Amateur Historian*, vol. VI, no. 7 (1965), pp. 235–242

Published Finding Aids

British National Archives, Government Publications, Sectional List 24 (revised annually)

Calendar of Charter Rolls, 1226–1516 (London, 1903–1927)

Calendar of Close Rolls, 1227–1509 (London, 1892–1963)

Calendar of Fine Rolls, 1272–1509 (London, 1911–1963)

Calendar of Inquisitions Miscellaneous, Henry III to Henry VII (London, 1916–1969)

Calendar of Inquisitions Post Mortem, Henry III to Henry VII (London, 1898–1974)

Calendar of Patent Rolls, 1216–1575 (London, 1891–1974)

'Calendarium Genealogicum: or Calendar of Heirs, extracted from the Inquisitions, temp. Edward II, 1–2 Edward II,' *Deputy Keeper's Report*, XXXII (1871), appendix 1, pp. 237–263; 3–4 Edward II, ed. J A C Vincent, *The Genealogist*, n.s. vols. 1–4, 6 (1884–1887, 1889)

Calendarium Genealogicum, Henry III and Edward I, ed. C Roberts (London, 1865)

Calendarium ... Inquisitionum ad quod Damnum, 1 Edward II to 38 Henry VI, ed. J Caley and R Lemon (London, 1803)

Calendarium Inquisitionum Post Mortem sive Escaetarum, ed. J Caley and J Bayley (London, 1806–1828)

Curia Regis Rolls, Richard I–26 Henry III (London, 1923–1979)

Descriptive Catalogue of Ancient Deeds, from before James I (London, 1890–1915)

Index of Inquisitions Post Mortem, Henry VIII to Charles I, PRO Lists and Indexes, vols. XXIII, XXVI, XXXI and XXXIII (London, 1907–1909)

Index of Persons named in Early Chancery Proceedings, 1385–1467, ed. C A Walmisley (Harleian Society, London, 1927–1928)

List and Index of Court Rolls, PRO Lists and Indexes, vol. VI, pt 1 (London, 1896)

'Inquisitiones post mortem temp Henry VIII to Charles I,' *The Genealogist*, n.s. vols. 9–19 (1893–1903), 25–34 (1908–1920)

Rotuli Curiae Regis, 6 Richard I–1 John, ed. F Palgrave (London, 1835)

G Wrottesley, *Pedigrees from the Plea Rolls, 1200–1500* (London, c. 1906)

Unpublished Finding Aids

PRO card index of records in print

List of Exchequer KR Subsidy Rolls, Lay Series (1925), TS

Index of names in Certificates of Residence, Edward VI–Charles II, TS

Plantagenet-Harrison notes from legal records, MS

Catalogue of Lists and Indexes, KB and CP, TS

Records

Chancery

C 53	Charter Rolls, 1 John to 8 Henry VIII
C 54	Close Rolls, 6 John to 1903
C 55	Close Rolls, Supplementary, 27 Henry III to 12 Henry VI
C 60	Fine Rolls, 1 John to 23 Charles I
C 66	Patent Rolls, 3 John to 9 George VI
C 132	Inquisitions Post Mortem: Henry III
C 133	Inquisitions Post Mortem: Edward I
C 134	Inquisitions Post Mortem: Edward II
C 135	Inquisitions Post Mortem: Edward III
C 136	Inquisitions Post Mortem: Richard II
C 137	Inquisitions Post Mortem: Henry IV
C 138	Inquisitions Post Mortem: Henry V
C 139	Inquisitions Post Mortem: Henry VI
C 140	Inquisitions Post Mortem: Edward IV
C 141	Inquisitions Post Mortem: Richard III
C 142	Inquisitions Post Mortem: Henry VII to Charles II
C 143	Inquisitions ad quod damnum, Henry III to Richard III
C 145	Inquisitions, Miscellaneous, 3 Henry III to 2 Richard III
C 146	Ancient Deeds, Series C, before 1603
C 147	Ancient Deeds, Series CC, before 1603
C 148	Ancient Deeds, Series CS, before 1603

Court of Common Pleas

CP 25	Feet of Fines, Henry II to 2 Victoria
CP 40	Plea Rolls, 1 Edward I to 38 Victoria

Palatinate of Durham
DURH 12   Feet of Fines, 1535–1834

Exchequer
E 115   Certificates of Residence, Edward VI to Charles II
E 136   Escheators' Accounts, Henry III to James I
E 149   Inquisitions Post Mortem, Henry III to Richard III
E 150   Inquisitions Post Mortem, Henry VII to James I
E 151   Inquisitions ad quod damnum, Henry III to Henry VI
E 152   Enrolments of Inquisitions, Edward I to Henry VIII
E 179   Subsidy Rolls, c. Henry II to William and Mary

Court of King's Bench
KB 26   Plea (Curia Regis) Rolls, 5 Richard I to 56 Henry III

VI Sources of help

The PRO does not undertake genealogical research, but will do brief searches for wills, etc., if supplied with sufficient information. If you wish someone to do a full search on your behalf an agent can be recommended but, after that, the arrangement between yourself and the agent will be of a purely private nature. The Association of Genealogists and Record Agents will also put you in touch with an accredited researcher. If you have sound reasons for believing that your family is 'armigerous' (entitled to bear a coat of arms) you should enquire of the Officer-in-Waiting at the College of Arms.

The Society of Genealogists has a genealogical library and a number of very useful indexes. It is open to members and to anyone else on a daily fee-paying basis.

The Historical Manuscripts Commission will provide information about the whereabouts of private papers.

VII Useful addresses

Alberta Genealogical Society
  Box 3151
  Edmonton T5J 2G7
  Canada

Fr. Godfrey Anstruther, O.P.
  1 Cliftsea Gore
  Leigh on Sea
  Essex SS9 1NG

Army Museums Ogilby Trust
  Ministry of Defence (Army)
  85 Whitehall,
  London SW1A 2NP

Army Records Centre
  Bourne Avenue
  Hayes
  Middx UB3 1RS

Association of Genealogists and Record
Agents
  Honorary Secretary
  80 Pollard Road
  London N20 0UD

Audin, Mme M.
  37 Rue La Quintinie
  75015 Paris
  France

Australian Genealogists, Society of
  Richmond Villa
  120 Kent Street
  Observatory Hill
  Sydney NSW 2000

Baptist Historical Society
  Baptist Union Library
  4 Southampton Row
  London WC1B 4AB

British Information Services
  845 Third Avenue
  New York
  NY 10022
  U.S.A.

British Columbia Genealogical Society
  The Library
  Langham College
  100W 49th Avenue
  Vancouver V5Y 2Z6
  Canada

British Library, Reference Division,
  Great Russell Street
  London WC1B 3DG

British Red Cross Society
  The Secretary
  9 Grosvenor Crescent
  London SW1X 7E1

Canterbury Cathedral Archives and
Library
  The Precincts
  Canterbury CT1 2EG

Capital Taxes Office
  Minford House
  Rockley Road
  London W14 0DF

Catholic Central Library
47 Francis St
London SW1P 1DN

Catholic Record Society
c/o Miss R. Rendel
114 Mount St
London W1Y 6AH

Centraal Bureau vor Genealogie
Nassaulaan, 18
Den Haag
Holland

Central Criminal Court
Courts' Administrator
Old Bailey
London EC4M 7EH

Chaplain of the Fleet
Ministry of Defence
Lacon House
Theobalds Road
London WC1X 8RY

Church of Jesus Christ of Latter Day
Saints
Hyde Park Chapel
64 Exhibition Road
London SW7 2PA

Civil Service Department
Alencon Link
Basingstoke
Hants RG21 1JB.

College of Arms
Queen Victoria Street
London EC4V 4BT

Corporation of London Record Office
Guildhall
London EC2P 2EJ

Department of Health and Social
Security
Schofield Mills
Brunswick Street
Nelson
Lancs BB9 0HU

District Probate Registries
Cavendish House
Waterloo Street
Birmingham B2 5PS

28 Richmond Place
Brighton BN2 2NA

4th Floor
37–41 Prince Street
Bristol BS1 4PX

15 Museum Street
Ipswich IP1 1HG

Devereux House
East Parade
Leeds LS1 2BA

Family Researchers Ltd
9 Gloucester Road
Bagshot
Surrey GU19 5LT

Federation of Family History Societies
General Secretary
96 Beaumont Street,
Milehouse,
Plymouth PL2 3AQ

Genealogical Society of South Africa
40 Haylett Street
Strand
Capetown
South Africa

Genealogical Society of Utah
50 East North Temple
Salt Lake City
Utah 84150
U.S.A.

General Register Office (CA Section)
  Titchfield
  Fareham
  Hants PO15 5RU

General Register Office
  Office of Population Censuses and
  Surveys
  St Catherine's House
  10 Kingsway
  London WC2B 6JP

General Registry
  Finch Road
  Douglas
  Isle of Man

Greater London Record Office
  County Hall
  London SE1 7PB

The Greffe
  Royal Court House
  St Peter Port
  Guernsey, C.I.

Guildhall Library
  Aldermanbury
  London EC2P 2EJ

Historical Manuscripts Commission
  Quality House
  Quality Court
  Chancery Lane
  London WC2A 1HF

Home Office
  Lunar House
  40 Wellesley Road
  Croydon CR9 2BY

The Honourable Society of
Cymmrodorion
  118 Newgate Street
  London EC1A 7AE

Huguenot Library
  University College
  Gower St
  London WC1E 6BT

Huguenot Society
  Miss I Scouloudi, Honorary
  Secretary
  67 Victoria Road
  London W8 5RH

Huguenot Society of Germany
  Geschaftstelle des deutschen
  Hugenotten-Vereins
  Postfach 35
  3305 Obersichte
  uber Brauschweig
  W. Germany

Imperial War Museum
  Lambeth Road
  London SE1 6HZ

The Archivist
  International Red Cross
  British Red Cross Training Centre
  Barnett Hill
  Wonersh
  Guildford
  Surrey GU1 3PJ

India Office Library and Records
  Foreign and Commonwealth Office
  197 Blackfriars Road
  London SE1 8NG

Irish Genealogical Society of Great
Britain
  c/o F B Payton
  The Challoner Club
  59–61 Pont Street
  London SW1 0BD

Jewish Museum
  Woburn House
  Upper Woburn Place
  London WC1H 0ED

John Rylands University Library
   Oxford Road
   Manchester M13 9PP

Judicial Greffe
   The States' Building
   Royal Square
   St Helier
   Jersey, C.I.

Lambeth Palace Library
   London SE1 7JU

HM Land Registry
   Lincoln's Inn Fields
   London WC2A 3PH

Manx Museum Library
   Kingswood Grove
   Douglas
   Isle of Man

Maritime History Group
   Memorial University of
   Newfoundland
   St John's
   Newfoundland
   Canada

Methodist Connexional Archivist
   c/o The Property Division
   Central Hall
   Oldham Street
   Manchester M1 1JQ

The Mocatta Library
   University College
   Gower Street
   London WC1E 6BT

National Army Museum
   Royal Hospital Road
   London SW3 4HT

National Genealogical Society
   1921, Sunderland Place N.W.
   Washington D.C. 20036
   U.S.A.

National Library of Wales
   Aberystwyth SY23 3BU

National Maritime Museum
   Greenwich
   London SE10 9NF

Naval Personnel Records
   Room 2007 0S9(a)
   Ministry of Defence
   Empress State Building
   London SW6 1TR

New Zealand Society of Genealogists
   PO Box 8795
   Symonds Street
   Auckland
   New Zealand

Norfolk Record Office
   Central Library
   Norwich NR2 1NJ

Ontario Genealogical Society
   Box 66
   Stn. Q
   Toronto M4T 2L7
   Canada

Presbyterian Historical Society of
England
   86 Tavistock Place
   London WC1H 9RR

Presbyterian Historical Society of
Northern Ireland
   Church House
   Fisherwick Place
   Belfast BT1 6DU

Principal Registry of the Family
Division
   Somerset House
   Strand
   London WC2R 1LA

Public Archives of Canada
  395 Wellington Street
  Ottawa 4
  Ontario K1A 0N3
  Canada

Public Record Office of Ireland
  Four Courts
  Dublin

Public Record Office of Northern
Ireland
  66 Balmoral Avenue
  Belfast BT9 6NY

Registrar General of Ireland
  Custom House
  Dublin

Registrar General of Northern Ireland
  Fermanagh House
  Ormeau Avenue
  Belfast BT2 8HX

Registrar General of Scotland
  New Register House
  Princes Street
  Edinburgh EH1 3YT

Registrar General of Shipping and
Seamen
  Llantrisant Road
  Llandaff
  Cardiff CF5 2YS

Registry of Deeds
  Henrietta Street
  Dublin

Religious Society of Friends
  The Librarian
  Friends' House
  Euston Road
  London NW1 2BJ

RAF Personnel Management Centre
  Eastern Avenue
  Barnwood
  Gloucester GL4 7AN

Royal Artillery Record and Manning
Office
  Imphal Barracks
  York YO1 4HD

Royal Courts of Justice
  Strand
  London WC2A 2LL

Royal Marines' Drafting and Record
Office
  HMS *Centurion*
  Grange Road
  Portsmouth PO13 9XA

Salvation Army
  (The Investigating Officer)
  110–112 Middlesex Street
  London E1 7HY

Scottish Record Office
  PO Box 36
  HM General Register House
  Edinburgh EH1 3YY

Scottish Tartans Society
  Davidson House
  Drummond Street
  Comrie
  Crieff
  Perthshire

Society of Genealogists
  37 Harrington Gardens
  London SW7 4JX

Southampton City Record Office
  Civic Centre
  Southampton SO9 4XL

Spanish and Portuguese Synagogue
  9 Lauderdale Road
  Maida Vale
  London W9 1LT

United Synagogue, Offices of the
  Alder House
  Woburn House
  Upper Woburn Place
  London WC1H 0ED

Dr Williams's Library
  14 Gordon Square
  London WC1H 0AG

The Weiner Library
  4 Devonshire Street
  London W1N 2BH

Appendix
How to find a record of a birth or baptism

i   Read the FIRST question.

ii   Answer 'yes' or 'no' to it, and then read the item to which you are referred.

iii   Carry on in this way reading ONLY the items you are instructed to read.

iv   Some items are instructions for searching. If the search is unsuccessful continue with the items to which you are referred.

1	Was the birth in England or Wales?	YES	*read* 28
		NO	*read* 2
2	Was the birth in Scotland?	YES	*read* 3
		NO	*read* 4
3	Consult records in General Registry, Edinburgh.	UNSUCCESSFUL	*read* 85
4	Was the birth in Ireland?	YES	*read* 5
		NO	*read* 10
5	Was the birth before 1 January 1922?	YES	*read* 8
		NO	*read* 6
6	Was the birth in Southern Ireland?	YES	*read* 9
		NO	*read* 7
7	Consult General Register Office, Belfast.	UNSUCCESSFUL	*read* 85
8	Was the birth after 1864?	YES	*read* 9
		NO	*read* 85
9	Consult General Register Office, Dublin.	UNSUCCESSFUL	*read* 85
10	Was the birth in India, Burma, Aden, St Helena, South-East Asia?	YES	*read* 11
		NO	*read* 12
11	Consult India Office Records.	UNSUCCESSFUL	*read* 13
12	Was the birth elsewhere in the Commonwealth?	YES	*read* 13
		NO	*read* 14
13	Consult registers in country of birth. See: General Register Office, *Abstract of arrangements respecting registration of births, marriages and deaths in the United Kingdom and the other countries of the British Commonwealth* ... (London, 1952).	UNSUCCESSFUL	*read* 19

14 Was the birth elsewhere abroad?	YES	*read* 15
	NO	*read* 22
15 Were the parents British?	YES	*read* 17
	NO	*read* 16
16 Consult immigration records in the Public Record Office.	UNSUCCESSFUL	*read* 85
17 Was the birth in St Petersburg, Russia, 1818–1940?	YES	*read* 18
	NO	*read* 19
18 Search RG 4/4605 in the Public Record Office.	UNSUCCESSFUL	*read* 19
19 Consult registers of births overseas, RG 32–36 in the Public Record Office.	UNSUCCESSFUL	*read* 20
20 Consult Bishop of London's Registers at Guildhall Library, London.	UNSUCCESSFUL	*read* 21
21 Consult miscellaneous registers at Lambeth Palace Library.	UNSUCCESSFUL	*read* 85
22 Was the birth at sea?	YES	*read* 23
	NO	*read* 27
23 Were the parents British?	YES	*read* 29
	NO	*read* 24
24 Was the birth after 1854?	YES	*read* 25
	NO	*read* 85
25 Was the ship British?	YES	*read* 26
	NO	*read* 85
26 Consult records of the Registrar of Shipping and Seamen in the Public Record Office.	UNSUCCESSFUL	*read* 85
27 Was the birth in a British aircraft?	YES	*read* 29
	NO	*read* 85
28 Was the birth before 1 July 1837?	YES	*read* 30
	NO	*read* 29
29 Consult records in General Register Office.	UNSUCCESSFUL	*read* 85
30 Was the birth after 1538?	YES	*read* 31
	NO	*read* 85
31 Is the place of birth known or assumed?	YES	*read* 47
	NO	*read* 32
32 Is the residence in 1841, 1851, 1861 or 1871 known?	YES	*read* 33
	NO	*read* 34
33 Consult census records in the Public Record Office.	UNSUCCESSFUL	*read* 34
34 Did the person serve subsequently in the British Army?	YES	*read* 35
	NO	*read* 36
35 Consult records of military service in the Public Record Office.	UNSUCCESSFUL	*read* 36

36 Did the person serve subsequently in the Royal Navy?	YES NO	*read 37* *read 38*
37 Consult records of naval service in the Public Record Office.	UNSUCCESSFUL	*read 38*
38 Did the person serve subsequently in the Army, Marine or Civil Service in India or with the East India Company?	YES NO	*read 39* *read 40*
39 Consult India Office Records.	UNSUCCESSFUL	*read 40*
40 Did the person serve subsequently in the Merchant Navy?	YES NO	*read 41* *read 42*
41 Consult Records of the Registrar General of Shipping and Seamen in the Public Record Office.	UNSUCCESSFUL	*read 42*
42 Did the person serve subsequently in the British Civil Service?	YES NO	*read 43* *read 45*
43 Was he appointed after 1855?	YES NO	*read 44* *read 45*
44 Consult Civil Service Department.	UNSUCCESSFUL	*read 45*
45 Did the person subsequently emigrate?	YES NO	*read 46* *read 85*
46 Consult emigration records in the Public Record Office.	UNSUCCESSFUL	*read 85*
47 Is the religious denomination of the person or his parents known?	YES NO	*read 60* *read 48*
48 Was the person born at the British Lying-in Hospital Holborn?	YES NO	*read 49* *read 50*
49 Consult RG 8/52–66 in the Public Record Office.	UNSUCCESSFUL	*read 50*
50 Was the person baptised in the Fleet or King's Bench Prisons, Mayfair Chapel or the Mint?	YES NO	*read 51* *read 52*
51 Consult RG 7 in the Public Record Office.	UNSUCCESSFUL	*read 84*
52 Was the person baptised in Greenwich Hospital?	YES NO	*read 53* *read 54*
53 Consult RG 4/1669, 1670, 1677, 1678 in the Public Record Office.	UNSUCCESSFUL	*read 84*
54 Was the person baptised in Chelsea Hospital?	YES NO	*read 55* *read 56*
55 Consult RG 4/4330, 4387 in the Public Record Office.	UNSUCCESSFUL	*read 84*
56 Was the person baptised in one of the Chapels Royal?	YES NO	*read 57* *read 58*

57	Consult RG 8/110 in the Public Record Office.	UNSUCCESSFUL	*read* 84
58	Was the person baptised in Somerset House Chapel?	YES NO	*read* 59 *read* 84
59	Consult RG 8/109 in the Public Record Office.	UNSUCCESSFUL	*read* 84
60	Was the person a member of a Foreign Protestant Church?	YES NO	*read* 61 *read* 64
61	Consult RG 4 and RG 8 in the Public Record Office.	UNSUCCESSFUL	*read* 62
62	Consult Foreign Protestant Registers in the Guildhall Library, London.	UNSUCCESSFUL	*read* 63
63	Consult the Huguenot Society	UNSUCCESSFUL	*read* 84
64	Was the person a member of a Russian Orthodox church?	YES NO	*read* 65 *read* 66
65	Consult RG 8/111–304 in the Public Record Office.	UNSUCCESSFUL	*read* 84
66	Was the person a Quaker (Religious Society of Friends)?	YES NO	*read* 67 *read* 69
67	Consult RG 6 and RG 8 in the Public Record Office.	UNSUCCESSFUL	*read* 68
68	Consult the Religious Society of Friends.	UNSUCCESSFUL	*read* 84
69	Was the person a Methodist or Wesleyan?	YES NO	*read* 70 *read* 73
70	Was the person born in or around London?	YES NO	*read* 71 *read* 77
71	Was the person born after 1818?	YES NO	*read* 72 *read* 77
72	Consult RG 4/4677–4680, RG 5/162–207 in the Public Record Office.	UNSUCCESSFUL	*read* 77
73	Was the person a member of some other protestant nonconformist church?	YES NO	*read* 74 *read* 78
74	Was the person born in or around London?	YES NO	*read* 75 *read* 77
75	Was the person born after 1742?	YES NO	*read* 76 *read* 77
76	Consult RG 4/4658–4676, RG 5/1–161 in the Public Record Office.	UNSUCCESSFUL	*read* 77
77	Consult RG 4 and RG 8 in the Public Record Office.	UNSUCCESSFUL	*read* 84
78	Was the person a Roman Catholic?	YES NO	*read* 79 *read* 81

79 Consult RG 4 in the Public Record Office.	UNSUCCESSFUL	*read* 80
80 Consult records of Roman Catholic churches held locally.	UNSUCCESSFUL	*read* 84
81 Was the person Jewish?	YES NO	*read* 82 *read* 83
82 Consult Synagogue records preserved locally or the Mormon Computer File Index.	UNSUCCESSFUL	*read* 85
83 Was the person a member of the Church of England (Anglican)?	YES NO	*read* 84 *read* 85
84 Consult Parish Registers held locally.	UNSUCCESSFUL	*read* 85
85 Take expert advice: e.g. of the Society of Genealogists.		

Public Record Office Museum Pamphlets

Facsimiles of documents etc., with introductory notes.

Public Record Office Handbooks

Her Majesty's Stationery Office

Government Bookshops

49 High Holborn, London WC1V 6HB
13a Castle Street, Edinburgh EH2 3AR
41 The Hayes, Cardiff CF1 1JW
Brazennose Street, Manchester M60 8AS
Southey House, Wine Street, Bristol BS1 2BQ
258 Broad Street, Birmingham B1 2HE
80 Chichester Street, Belfast BT1 4JY

*Government Publications are also available
through booksellers*

Printed in England by McCorquodale Printers Ltd., London
Dd696378 C900